ABOUT THE AUTHOR

David started woodworking at an early age by using the drill press in his father's woodworking buisness to drill holes in blocks of scrap wood on Saturdays. He eventually started actually building recognizable items as he worked with and for his father through high school and college.

A degree in English Literature shifted his sights to journalism, but he was never far away from woodworking, eventually opening his own custom woodworking shop for a few years.

In the mid-90's he found a blending of both worlds, going to work for *Popular Woodworking* magazine as an editor, builder and tool reviewer.

He took on a side job as host of the DIY Network's Tools & Techniques (still playing somewhere out in space), and in the beginning of the new millenia he started working at his current position as Executive Editor with Popular Woodworking Books.

David lives in Cincinnati, Ohio and still enjoys checking out a new tool, whenever possible. You can visit his web site at www.theshopofthecrafters.com.

ACKNOWLEDGEMENTS

As an author, whenever I refer to "my" book I always feel uncomfortable. While it certainly is my book, there are always others who deserve recognition for its creation.

First is to my family. My wife, Patti and all five kids, Dillon, Danielle, Shannon, Ben and Zach, who put up with my disappearing into the garage to build something. There were too many weekends lost to "the book" that could have been family time.

I'll again thank Patti, first for her love — then for her design direction and input on all the projects. Even if it was just a comforting "that looks great" (and there were many more in-depth discussions), her support through the project was extremely important; so I dedicate this book to her. Thank you, babe.

Thanks to Jim Stack, my editor, who I've known for over thirty years, in a few different roles. His patience and quiet support (and excellent illustration work) kept me from chewing my nails too far.

And to my designer Brian Roeth, again for patience and for allowing me to gently nudge the design, even though he knew where he was going.

Thanks also to my e-mail critic, Jeff Korbman, for his instightful read of the nearly-finished manuscript.

A big thank you to Steve and Kit for letting us use "the house of many rooms" as background for the opening photos.

And lastly, to my readers over the years, both with *Popular Woodworking Magazine*, and in earlier books. Your feedback, both positive and "corrective" gave me the recognition of the need for a book that offered time- and material-consious woodworking projects that still looked good. I hope this book serves as a thank you.

CONTENTS

NEW: BUNGALOW
NEW: BUNGALOW
ARTS & CRAFTS FURNITURE
SMITH AND VERTIKOFF
GREENE & GREENE: MASTERWORKS

INTRODUCTION

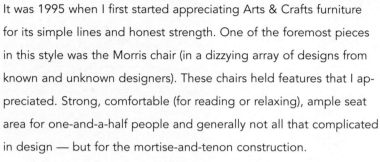

It was 1995 when I first started appreciating Arts & Crafts furniture for its simple lines and honest strength. One of the foremost pieces in this style was the Morris chair (in a dizzying array of designs from known and unknown designers). These chairs held features that I appreciated. Strong, comfortable (for reading or relaxing), ample seat area for one-and-a-half people and generally not all that complicated in design — but for the mortise-and-tenon construction.

So I built a couple. They lived up to my expectations, looked good and made me proud. Then fall entered my little part of southwest Ohio and I wanted to spend more time on my deck enjoying the crisp air and the beautiful colors (along with a good cigar and a nice glass of wine). And I wanted to be comfortable — like in my Morris chair. While white oak is actually a pretty sturdy outdoor wood, I wasn't in the mood to drag (let alone leave) my Morris chair outside. What to do?

Adirondack chairs for outdoor use, (both in plan form and for sale, completed) were in abundance. But I preferred the Morris, and outdoor plans were sorely missing for them. But hey, I'm a woodworker, so this was a challenge that sounded like fun. I started with the overall dimensions from one of Gus Stickley's slant-arm chairs (that I found particularly comfortable) and tried to figure out how to build one using 1x pine from the home center store. I've built a few variations of that outdoor Morris since then, (each better, I hope) but they all sit well, are easy to make (just a screw gun, miter saw and a jigsaw) and with a few cans of spray paint, I have to say they look pretty good!

Why would I, as a woodworker, buy lumber from the home center stores? Couldn't I find better quality wood at a better price, that only required a little preparation? That "preparation" (kiln dry, face, plane and dimension the lumber) means access to rough lumber, and a jointer, planer and table saw. Not all readers who would like to build furniture have access to the materials or tools. But almost everyone has access to a home center store. Even with the added expense, my Morris chair cost less than $75 for lumber. And today I can build one in under three hours, because I don't have to prepare the lumber. A fair trade in my book (which happens to be the one in your hands...).

As a woodworking editor, I frequently need to remember that not everyone building a project has the same experience, space or tools that I have. Many readers don't even want to be a woodworker. They just like to build an occasional project for around the house. They're not worried about mortise-and-tenon joinery and they don't own a thickness planer. These are the folks that I can help: The Weekend Woodworking Warrior.

Each of the projects in this book have been designed to use a minimum of tools. I've made some allowances for using a benchtop table saw, but most could be built with a jigsaw, miter saw, screws and glue. I've re-designed some classic furniture pieces (and designed a couple from scratch) to use only joinery that can be mastered in a couple of hours: biscuit joints, dowels, pocket screws and just plain screws.

The wood I've used for each project (dimensional lumber in red oak, birch, poplar or pine) is available at Lowe's or Home Depot. I've also added some plywood to avoid having to glue up solid panels. Gus would have done it! With some judicious staining, and painting, I feel that the designs retain much of the charm of the originals, while making a finished piece of furniture accessible to even the most inexperienced woodworker.

I hope you enjoy the convenience of these modified Arts & Crafts classics, and also enjoy many years of comfort and use of all that you build.

— David Thiel

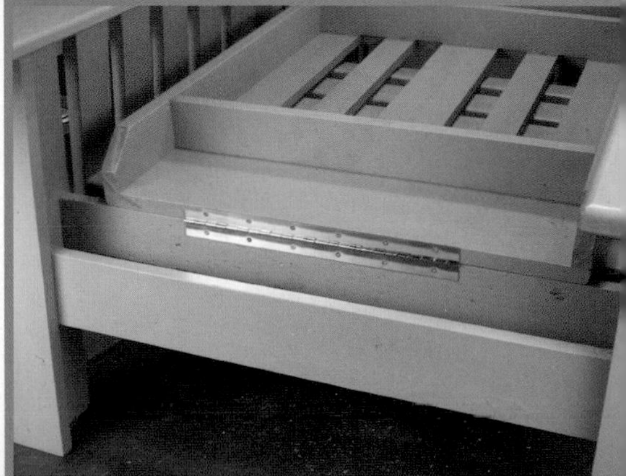

THE SECRET TO EASY FURNITURE MAKING

1

When a woodworker looks at a completed piece of furniture, they almost automatically start deconstructing it in their head. Are the shelves of a bookcase captured by a groove cut in the sides? Do the stretchers on a table have tenons that are mortised into the legs? These are the details of furniture making that make woodworking a "skill". And there's nothing wrong with that.

But what if you drill a recessed hole in the leg, drive a screw into the stretcher and glue a wooden plug into the hole? The strength created by the screw joint is still good. The plug will be sanded flush and may show a little. But "expressed joinery" is part of the culture of Arts & Crafts furniture. This may be stretching a little, but what is gained is a serviceable replacement for hours of work, and possibly years of experience. Sound good? Follow me...

THE WOOD

As I mentioned in the introduction, one of the secrets to easy furniture-making is not having to prepare the wood. And it's not just the machining of the wood, it's the finding of the wood. The most experienced woodworkers will have sources for rough lumber that they've cultivated over years. From barns out in a field, to a local sawmill that sells wholesale, they can purchase quality, kiln-dried rough lumber at very good prices.

But these resources aren't generally available to the average Weekend Woodworker. If they want to buy lumber they end up at a specialty woodworking store where the prices (though appropriate) are significantly higher than those mentioned above. Part of that price increase is because the wood has likely been joined, planed and sized for building. That costs money.

The specialty woodworking stores are a reasonable option for many hardwood species, and if you're interested in building any of the projects in this book in a different hardwood, then I'd recommend you check out Rockler (www.rockler.com) or Woodcraft (www.woodcraft.com) for a location near you.

On the other hand, if you're fine with a project that offers quick and satisfactory results, then Lowe's, Home Depot, Menards and others will have pine, poplar and red oak machined to size and ready to handle your needs.

You should spend some time checking the lumber in the store to look for the straightest, best boards in the racks. You may not always find everything you need, but by knowing the lengths and uses of the finished pieces, you can argue that a slightly bowed board — when cut into three lengths — will do just fine. You should also take a look at the grain of the boards, with the project-of-the-day in mind. A single board of good color and grain pattern makes a fine tabletop. If you have to mix boards for a panel or top that isn't a good match, the look will be diminished.

THE JOINERY

By removing some of the machinery normally used to prepare the wood, we've certainly made the process easier, but we've also caused some concerns. By working with "factory" edges (the edges prepared prior to sale) we're trusting that the edges are square and true — not always the case. As you lay out your pieces for any of the projects, you'll want to check the mating edges for the best fit. Some will be good, others may have a bow, or a defect that will be visible.

If the joint needs improvement, we are, (by using only a select group of tools), pushed toward using a hand plane to clean up the edge. This may sound like a painful step in the wrong direction for easy furniture making. However, if you learn to simply true an edge with a bench plane, you'll save yourself hours of disappointment over the years. I'm not talking about becoming a hand tool woodworker, but simply learn to true an edge. There are dozens of books and online videos that can give you the simple basics for this task.

Biscuits, or plate joinery, can be used for end grain and long grain joinery as shown here in a flat glue-up. They can also be used in right-angle joinery, providing strength and alignment.

A simple countersink/pilot drill bit allows you to pre-drill a clearance hole to avoid wood splitting and makes a convenient hole to receive a wood plug, hiding the screw. One bit for two jobs.

With reasonably true edges, we need to find a way to join our pieces. For tabletops and panels, boards need to be joined long-edge to long-edge. This is a very strong glue joint, and, with a couple of clamps is the simplest of joinery. However, if you wish to improve the ease of this glueup, adding biscuits to the joint allows you to align the surfaces of the board with a bit more accuracy than a free-hand glueup, and the biscuit remains hidden. It also reduces the amount of sanding needed to even out the surfaces of your panel.

For joining two pieces at a right angle we can use a couple of different methods. As shown at left, the use of a biscuit joint helps align the pieces for better accuracy and if you're joining short-grain pieces, biscuits will also add strength.

Basic screws are also an option. I prefer (and used on all of the projects) a coarse-thread drywall screw. They have thinner shanks, reducing the risk of splitting the wood, and they drive easily.

If the screw is in a place that is visible, a recessed hole (countersunk) makes it easy to glue a like-species plug in place that can be sanded flush to the surface. Not invisible, but certainly low profile.

Another joinery method I used on some of the projects are pocket screws. With a simple jig, drill and bits, right-angle and panel joinery can be created with a great deal of strength. This method is best used in a non-visible location, but there are also like-species plugs available to hide the pocket screws holes.

Nails. Yes, nails. Every now and then the old ways are the best. To hold a back in place, or to attach an awkward piece, sometimes a small brad nail is just the ticket. Set the nail head below the surface of the wood, add a little putty, sand and it's nearly invisible.

THE FINISH

I sanded all of the projects to a final 120 grit smoothness using a standard random orbit sander. I then made sure to break, or ease the sharp edges on all the pieces using the same grit sandpaper by hand. If you prefer, you can go higher with your finish grit, but there's a diminishing return for the effort much further than 150 grit.

Though I've used a wide variety of finishes over the years, I held to finishes that are available off the rack from Lowe's and Home Depot. Primarily Minwax products, I used standard wood stains and also some of their gel stains for a different affect. Gel stains don't penetrate the wood as deeply as regular stains, leaving the depth of color lighter.

I also used paint for most of the exterior projects, using a good exterior grade enamel that was brushed on, but also using some simple Krylon in a spray can for others.

Speaking of spray cans, most of the top coats for the stained projects were created using simple spray cans of lacquer finish. I generally opted for a semi-gloss finish. I won't tell you this is the least expensive top coat finish, but it sure is quick, and the results are pretty darn good.

One comment here. Do make sure you're working with lacquer, not urethane. Not that there's anything wrong with urethane, in fact it does provide a more durable finish than lacquer, but it's more difficult to apply evenly and takes days rather than minutes to dry. If you're not sure of the product, check the drying time on the can. If it's an hour or less, you're holding a can of lacquer.

USING THE TOOLS

2

All the clever designing to make these projects simple would mean nothing if I gave you a list of tools to use that you didn't own. The hard (and fun) part of the process for me has been to make each of the projects as accessible as possible, while still maintaining a decent look and solid construction. So, on the following pages is a discussion of the tools you likely have already, those that will be critical and those that would be handy, or even desirable. We'll also talk about some details about using each tool that will take out even more of the learning curve.

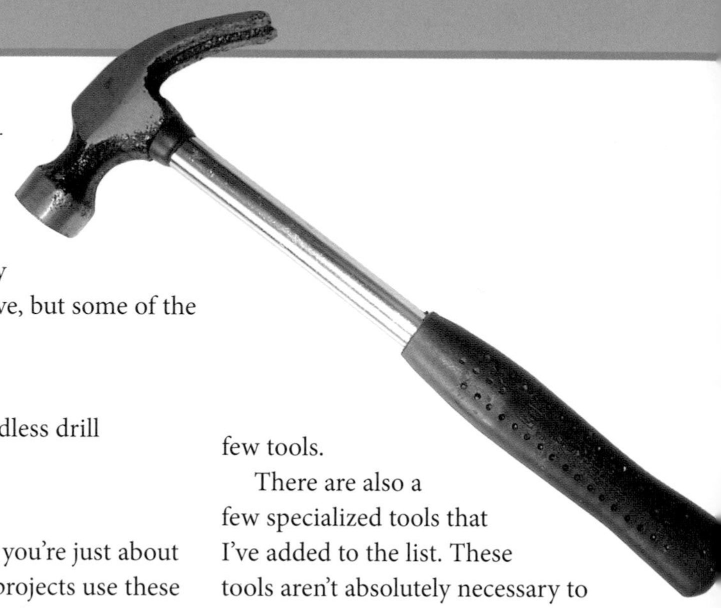

A LIKELY SHOP

The average homeowner, even if they aren't a woodworker, likely have a few tools around that will come in handy with these projects. Those listed below are common in most households:

- Hammer
- Screwdriver
- Tape measure
- Sandpaper
- Glue

If you're one of the millions of homeowners that handle their own home repairs, or if you happen to be one of the growing number of people who build the occasional weekend project, there's a pretty good chance you not only have the basics above, but some of the following:

- Circular saw
- Corded or cordless drill
- Drill bits
- Clamps

If that's the case, you're just about there. Many of the projects use these tools as the basis for their construction and can be built using only these few tools.

There are also a few specialized tools that I've added to the list. These tools aren't absolutely necessary to build the projects, but they can make things a little easier.

TABLE SAW

In designing the projects in this book I've worked to use the most common lumber types and sizes available at your local home center store.

The two biggies (Lowe's and Home Depot) price very similarly for these items, so while comparison shopping can be helpful (material quality may vary enough to make it worth the extra trip), you'll end up spending about the same in either store. The lumber is generally available in dimensional widths including:

- 1 × 3 (or ¾" × 2½")
- 1 × 4 (or ¾" × 3½")
- 1 × 6 (or ¾" × 5½")
- 1 × 8 (or ¾" × 7½")

All of these widths are available in 6', 8', and 10' lengths.

Back to the design. While I worked hard to use the widths as purchased, some of the designs just didn't work as well with stock sizes. I needed a nonexistent 1×5 (4½" wide) a few times to make things look better.

A 5½" board can be ripped to 4½" with a circular saw or jigsaw, and then cleaned up with a hand plane. However, a table saw can make this a much quicker process. Portable table saws range in price from $200 to $600. If you plan on making woodworking an ongoing hobby, you may want to consider purchasing a portable table saw. Ripping (cutting lengthwise) is only one of the many operations this tool can offer.

That said, if you're just building a couple of the projects from this book, a jigsaw and hand plane will probably do just fine.

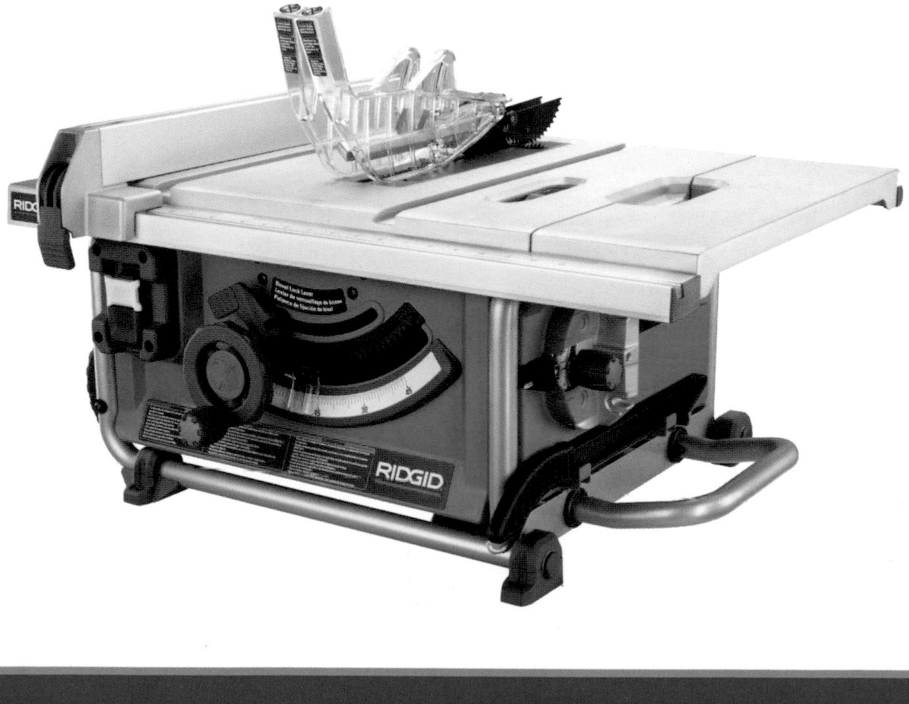

JIGSAW

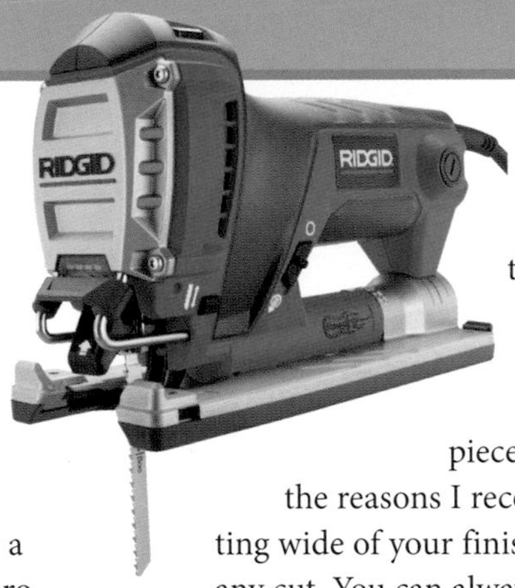

A jigsaw is one of the more versatile tools you can add to your shop. You can cut a fairly straight line with it, or cut circles or curves. You can buy a decent jigsaw for around $50, or a good one for $100. The pro models are priced around $150. Regardless of price, there are a few tips and bits of advice I want to give you to help you get the most from your jigsaw.

Whatever the quality of saw you purchase, there is one "habit" jigsaws have that you should be aware of. Because the blade is held by the tool only at the top, the end of the blade has a tendency to flex to the left or right during the cut. And depending on which side of the blade you keep against the "finished" side of your cut, the flex can change. Make a few test cuts with your saw so that you can anticipate this flex and won't undercut your piece. This is one of the reasons I recommend cutting wide of your finished line during any cut. You can always come back and clean up a rough cut, but if your cut is beveled on the underside, you won't have enough wood to clean up.

Most jigsaws have optional orbital action. This setting allows you to adjust the aggressiveness of the cut by pushing the tip of the blade forward-and-up rhythmically during the cut. When you're cutting a straight line through oak, this orbital action is a great benefit. However, when using the jigsaw to cut out a detailed shape, (such as the squares in the Hill House Entry Table), the orbital action will cause the cut on the underside of

your piece to continue further than where you see your cut from above. When doing this kind of detail work, set the orbital function to off, or "O" for a more accurate cut.

One other piece of advice when using a jigsaw. Even though they're a good tool for cutting curves, if the curve is a tight radius, the blade can bind between the walls of the cut and kick quite a bit. In these situations I prefer to cut relief cuts (see the picture above) tangential to the curve. This way, as you cut the curve, the waste pieces fall away and the blade doesn't bind or kick in the cut.

BISCUIT JOINER

The biscuit joiner, or plate joiner, is a portable power tool that prices between $130 and $200. What it does is cut a slot in two corresponding pieces of wood that then accept a wooden football-shaped disc (the biscuit). With glue and clamping time, the biscuit joint is a modern

equivalent of a wooden spline — a concept that has been used in woodworking for many centuries. I've used biscuit joints throughout the projects to replace a number of more complicated joinery techniques. I strongly recommend this tool as a great addition to the simplified wood shop.

As for using a biscuit joiner, it's really one of the simplest tools. An adjustable fence guides the height (measuring from the face of the material you're working on, see the photo at right) down along the edge where the pocket will be cut. The fence adjusts to cut the pocket in the center of the edge (the optimal location) and can adjust for a wide variety of material thicknesses.

Another adjustment controls the depth of the cut, which relates directly to the size of the biscuit being used. The most common biscuit sizes are #10 and #20. I've used #10 biscuits throughout the book to keep things simple. Other than that, just make alignment marks on both your pieces and go to work!

TRIM ROUTER

Entire books have been written about the benefits and use of routers in the wood shop. These are extraordinarily helpful tools that can create grooves and rabbets (technically half a groove) to name just a few of the profiles available by using different bits. Not too long ago, adding a router to your shop could be a pricey prospect, but today there's a whole new category of powerful, pint-sized routers that are honestly all you need for the majority of woodworking applications. These trim routers (about $100) are also easier to handle during operation, with only one hand necessary to guide the tool.

If you've never used a router before, there are a couple of pieces of advice that will prove useful. First, there is a proper direction when using the router. If you look at the router from above and imagine that the base is the face of a clock, the router should be run against the wood in a counter-clockwise manner. Or, if the piece is straight, the piece of wood should be to the left of the tool, and you should be pushing the router away from your body. If you happen to run the router the opposite direction, it's called climb-cutting. The danger in this is that the rotation of the bit against the wood will work like a wind-up car when you set it down, moving the router quickly against the wood.

Another important thing to remember is to keep the base of the router flat against the surface of the wood. Because a router is taller than it is wide, the center of gravity is pretty high. Should the router tip slightly during the cut it will change the shape/angle of the profile that you are cutting.

Along those same lines, where you stop and start a cut can be important. The bit is centered in the base, and you can't always see exactly where (or when) the bit contacts the wood. If you are trying to run a profile along only one edge of a piece of wood and the bit comes in contact with the corner of the piece too early, you can start your profile on the adjacent edge. The same with ending your cut. So when placing the router in position to start your cut, center the body (9:00 position) of the router over the point where you want to start (or end) the cut. This takes a little practice, but is easy to learn.

COUNTERSINK

In general, drilling a clearance (or pilot) hole before inserting a screw is good advice. To add another layer, the bit I used throughout the book is a combination bit that cuts both a pilot hole and countersink hole at the same time. These bits come in different sizes to accommodate different diameter plugs. I used ⅜" plugs that covered my screws well, but also was small enough to be unobtrusive. One of the other little features of these bits is that the piloting bit can be adjusted for length, using an Allen wrench. This came in handy a couple of times when I needed to use a longer screw to provide more holding strength.

When drilling your holes, you will want to pay some attention to how deep you drill with the countersink part of the bit. If you use the entire length of the countersink, you may find that your plugs will not stop before seating below the surface of the wood. This defeats the purpose of the plug, so, test first to become familiar with how your tools work.

POCKET SCREWS

While I use countersunk screws with wood plugs in many of the projects, these aren't always the best way to attach pieces of wood, particularly because they are visible, even with the plugs. One other alternative is the use of pocket screws. Primarily the domain of the Kreg company, this "hidden screw" technology offers lots of opportunities to make quick, simple joints that hold up well. The basic starter tool runs around $40, with more versatile kits running around $100.

For joining pieces end-to-edge, long edge-to-long edge and even to for corners, a pocket screw can really simplify construction and speed things up. Faster? Yep, you don't have to use clamps to hold the pieces together while the glue dries. I like that!

And if you find that you're using a pocket screw in a place that will be visible, no problem. Plugs are available (as shown here) in a variety of wood species.

SPRAY LACQUER

While spray lacquer isn't exactly a tool, it does require a bit of explanation. Unlike a professional spray finishing system, the aerosol cans that are available from the home center stores put down a lighter coat of finish, and will require a bit more care in the application.

First, absolutely only apply spray lacquer in a well-ventilated area. It's gets pretty strong quickly. This advice would tend to send many of us outside (and that's where I try and do most of my spray finishing). However, spray lacquer is best applied in a moderate temperature (between 60° and 80° F) and high humidity can cause problems for even-drying. You'll also want to pay attention to which direction the wind (if any) is blowing.

When you spray you should start off of the edge of the piece and run past the edge on the opposite side. This will keep the finish from building too heavily as you start and stop. The spray should be applied in long, even stripes, overlapping the preceding stripe by about one-third to half. The spray tips don't apply an even concentration across the entire pattern, leaving the edges of the circle lighter than the center. By overlapping the stripes the pattern evens out.

While the can will recommend waiting a couple of hours between application, you can likely apply the next coat (two or three are likely necessary) sooner. After about 30 minutes carefully run you hand along the surface. If it's dry and not pliable (a little like leather) then you're ready to reapply. I've started using 0000 steel wool between coats with excellent success.

HORIZONTAL MIRROR

3

This is a very simple mirror frame that is reminiscent of hundreds of mirrors made by all the different Arts & Crafts manufacturers. Every catalog had at least a few mirror designs. Even today's manufacturers place a pretty high value on something that's so simple to create. So I think this is a pretty good first project for simplicity.

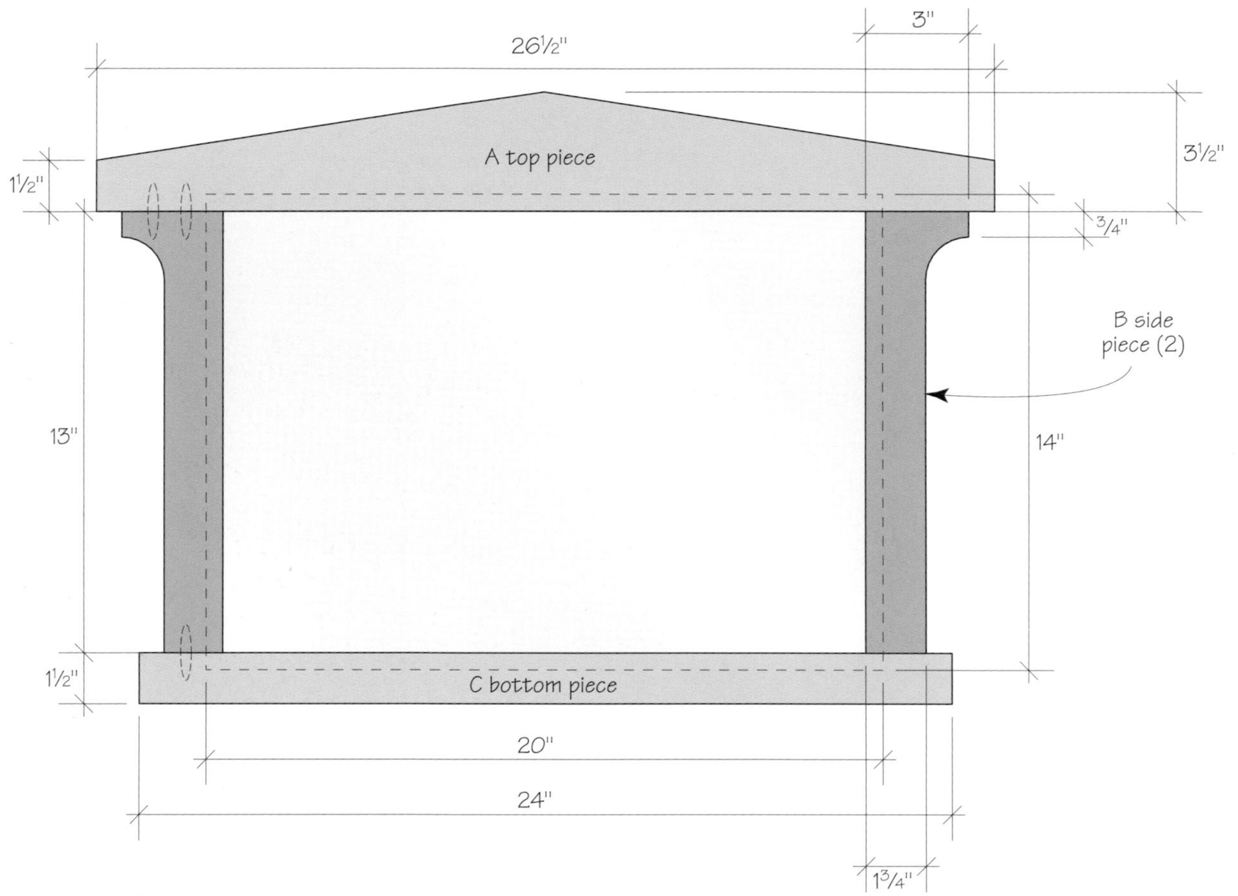

HORIZONTAL MIRROR • INCHES (MILLIMETERS)

REFERENCE	QUANTITY	PART	STOCK	THICKNESS	(mm)	WIDTH	(mm)	LENGTH	(mm)
A	1	top piece	oak	3/4	19	3 1/2	89	26 1/2	673
B	2	side pieces	oak	3/4	19	3	76	14	356
C	1	bottom piece	oak	3/4	19	1 1/2	38	24	610

1 Locating the proper spacing for the pocket screws coming up through the side pieces.

2 With the pocket screw locations figured out, it was quick work to cut the pockets. You might be tempted to cut the shapes, first, but working with the full piece is easier in the jig.

The frame is four pieces, in this case red oak. I was working with the smallest pieces of 1× material I could use to keep the price of materials very low. If you didn't have scraps available to build this frame, the materials would run you under $25 for one 1×4×8' piece and one 1×2×8' piece, and you'd have wood left over. Also, the mirror is a $10, ⅛" mirror for hanging on the back of a door. I've simply cut it to 20" in length (one cut) and designed the mirror frame to fit that size. If you've never cut a mirror, the internet offers a number of simple videos to walk you through this simple task.

Start out by cutting the top and two side pieces to length from the 1×4 piece. Leave them full width (3½") for now. Then cut the bottom piece to length from the 1×2.

The frame is assembled with pocket screws, though some of the locations need to be carefully placed. When I tried to space two pocket screws in the sides, running up into the top piece, I ran out of space to allow the "pocket" created by the pocket screw bit. I wanted two screws at that joint to keep the sides flat, and I was only using one screw at the bottom joint.

Another spacing complication was created by the ⅛" × ½" rabbet (a two-sided groove) on the inside edge of each side piece. We need that rabbet to hold the mirror.

After looking at things closer, I opted to cut the screw closest to center on the side piece, and the screw closest to the outside edge of the frame from the top piece. This caused a little visible nick on the top, back edge of the top pieces, but it's not visible once the mirror is hung.

With all the screw pockets cut, I turned to the shapes. I first marked the center of the top piece (13¼" from either end). Then measure down 2" on both ends and make a mark. Connect the dots to get the shape for the top piece. I used a jigsaw to rough out the shape, then followed that up with my bench plane.

Even though this is home center red oak, you will still find hints of the quarter-sawn ray flake that appears so commonly in original Arts & Crafts pieces. Lucky us!

To shape the two side pieces into what the Arts & Crafts folk call a corbel, I mark each piece 1¾" in from the center on the bottom edge, This is where our corbel terminates. It begins with a 1¼" radius curve (a protractor makes the curve easy to mark) at the top of each side, but held down ¾" from the top edge. Mark the shapes, on each piece, then grab your jigsaw.

With a little planning, cutting a curve with a jigsaw is easy. First, if you're using a jigsaw with orbital action, set it to zero so the blade cuts straight up-and-down. Before cutting the curve, I like to cut relief cuts into the curve, this way the scrap piece will fall away before the blade has a chance to bind in the curve. Much easier and safer.

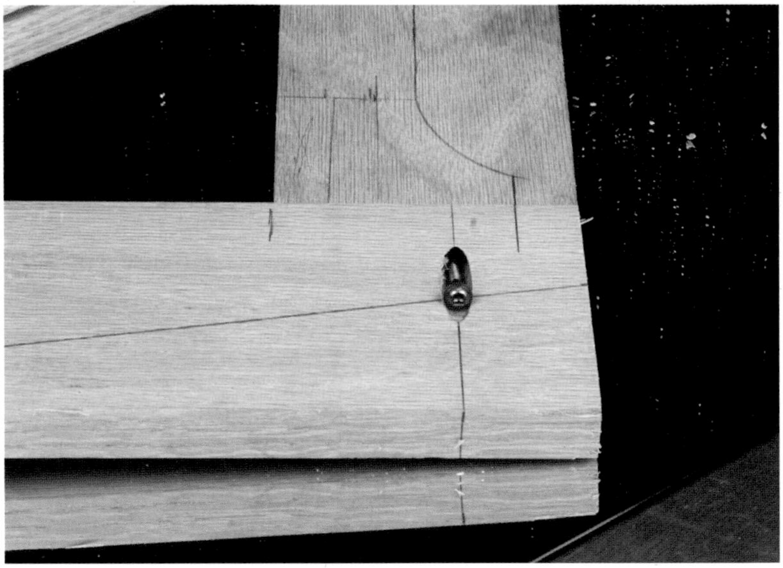

3 Two from below don't fit, so one screw needs to come from the top.

4 A jigsaw quickly cuts away the two waste sections from the top pieces. Stay a little wide of the mark to allow for cleanup.

5 Clean up with a few swipes of my bench plane. Who needs a table saw!?

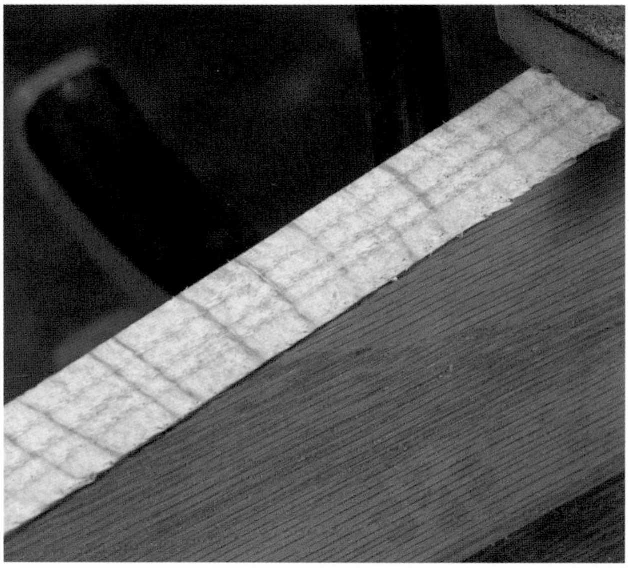

6 And look what the hand plane revealed; some nice ray flake on the top edge of the piece.

7 My relief cuts in the curve on the side pieces. These cuts make cutting the curve easier and safer.

8 With the pieces cleaned up, it looks the mirror frame is almost done. Almost...

After sanding the cuts on the side pieces (I used my random orbit sander for much of the cleanup), I was ready to screw the frame together. I did find a strong excuse for drilling a pilot hole for the screw going through the top piece and into the top of the corbel — splitting. Luckily a little glue and a clamp and I was able to fix the first piece. By drilling a pilot hole on the other side, the screw went in easily.

Screwing a frame together with pocket screws offers another benefit. No need for glue! You could glue the joint, but it's a bad joint for strength, and the glue just gets all over the place. The pocket screw is fine by itself.

To fit the piece of mirror into the frame, I cut a ⅛" × ½" rabbet on the inside of the frame using a rabbeting bit in my trim router. If you don't happen to have that size rabbeting bit (mine allows me to change bearings to adjust the width) you can adjust the mirror or frame sizes slightly to accommodate the rabbet size.

If you don't have a rabbeting bit of any kind, or even a trim router, then you can actually just mount the mirror flat to the back of the frame using mirror mounting clips. Your mirror will lean away from the wall a bit more because of the clips, but it is easier.

A good sanding over the entire piece with my random orbit sander and then a final swipe on all the edges with some 120-grit sandpaper and I was ready to apply a finish.

9 A split corner that I should have avoided by drilling a pilot hole for the screw.

10 With a pilot holed drilled on the other side, no splitting problems.

11 Another screw up from the bottom and the side is held tightly in place.

12 I used my trim router and a rabbeting bit to cut the rabbet for the mirror. The corners needed to be squared-off with a little hand chisel work.

13 The last step is to mount the mirror in place. I added a piece of cardboard from the mirror's packaging and used plastic screen door clips to hold the mirror and cardboard in place.

14 I used Minwax Aged Oak Gel Stain to color the piece (if you prefer a darker finish, choose a non-gel stain for better penetration) and topped the piece with a couple of coats of Deft Semi-gloss Spray Lacquer.

GAMBLE HOUSE MIRROR

4

Arts & Crafts mirrors are a popular accessory, and it's easy to see why. Beyond a standard mirror, each usually adds subtle elements to liven things up. This mirror (the original of which is from the Gamble House in Pasadena, CA) was designed to by hung by two leather straps from a plate rail high on the wall. The two "slots" are the location for the straps. If you choose to use this method, more power to you, but I think it also makes an interesting detail without the straps.

This frame could be made more simply, but the vertical sides are actually recessed back ⅛" from the front surfaces of the top and bottom pieces. This little detail makes the construction more involved, but adds a pleasant shadow line to the piece that makes it worth the effort.

The original mirror is made of solid mahogany, but Lowes and Home Depot still aren't stocking this beautiful wood (don't hold your breath). So I opted for poplar with a mahogany stain. Start building by cutting all the pieces to length.

To create the ⅛" offset, the two vertical pieces are rabbetted at both ends to allow them to slip slightly behind the horizontal pieces. While requiring a bit of accuracy, this was a fairly simple step using by benchtop table saw. If this tool isn't in your arsenal, I'd recommend a couple of cuts with a decent hand saw. Again, it'll take some accuracy with a hand tool, but the rabbet is hidden at the back of the piece, so perfect isn't necessary.

With the rabbets cut, I moved on to the "handles" on the top piece. Mark the locations of the waste areas, then grab your jigsaw and start cutting. I've outlined in the captions what I consider to be good technique for making this type of cut with a jigsaw.

The offset, or recessed look of this mirror is something I love, and the joinery to make it happen isn't too tough, but, when you stop to think about adding

1 Start by cutting the four pieces to length, then mark the top and bottom ends of both sides for the 1½" × ⅝" rabbets that will lap behind the horizontal pieces.

2 Cutting these rabbets requires a certain amount of accuracy, so it's a good idea to start by checking the squareness of your saw's miter gauge to the blade. As you can see, I'm out by a 1/16" or so.

GAMBLE HOUSE MIRROR • INCHES (MILLIMETERS)

REFERENCE	QUANTITY	PART	STOCK	THICKNESS	(mm)	WIDTH	(mm)	LENGTH	(mm)
A	2	sides	poplar	¾	19	2½	64	23*	584
B	1	bottom	poplar	¾	19	2½	64	17	432
C	1	top	poplar	¾	19	3½	89	20	584
D	1	mirror		⅛	3	11	279	22	559

*Rabbeted on one long edge and both ends.

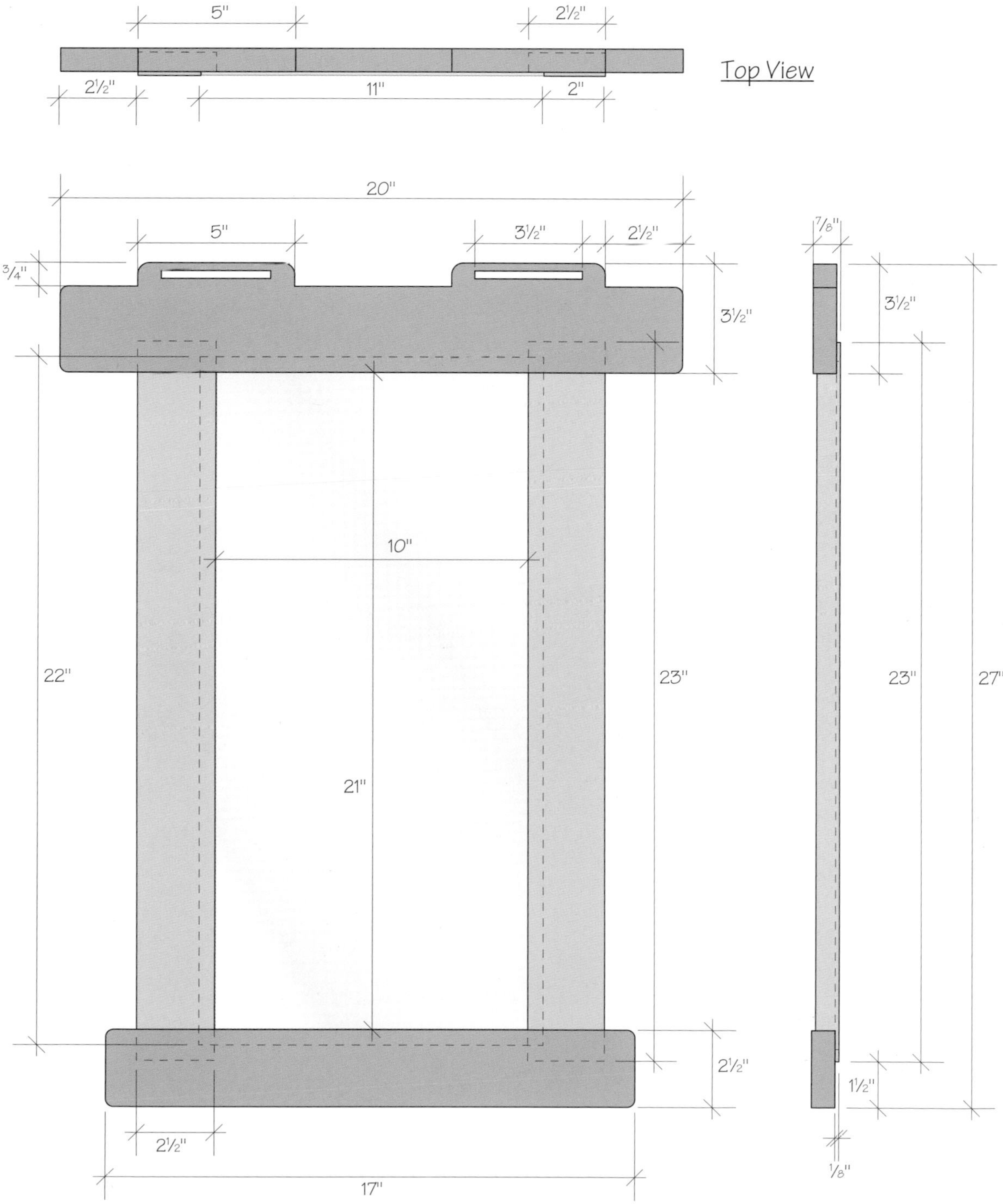
5"
2½"
Top View
2½"
11"
2"
20"
5"
3½"
2½"
¾"
3½"
10"
22"
23"
21"
2½"
2½"
17"
⅞"
3½"
23"
27"
1½"
⅛"

a mirror (or a picture and glass, for that matter), the offset again causes difficulties. To allow the mirror to fit tight against the frame without a gap, you need to bring the back surfaces in line again. I accomplished this by added a ⅛" × ½" rabbet on the inside back edge of only the two side pieces using my table saw. If a table saw isn't an option, a rabbeting plane will do, or a router (with, or without a router table) could be pressed into service.

To add the slots for the leather straps, I ended up using my biscuit jointer (as one of the available tools). This took some thinking, but worked out significantly better than expected, and much better than a test slot that I tried to create using a chisel and mallet (see photos 13 & 14).

With all the cutting complete, I got out my trim router and used an ⅛" roundover bit to ease all the edges of the pieces. I then sanded the piece, and again added some more rounding to the corners of the top and bottom horizontal pieces.

For a finish I started to use a gel stain, but because of the grain of the poplar, it wouldn't darken up enough to make me happy. So I switched to a penetrating stain, using a traditional mahogany stain. A couple of coats of a satin, spray lacquer (from a can … I love it!) gave the final appearance.

3 A little adjustment to the miter gauge will make the assembly easier.

4 Next, set the height of the blade to ⅝" to make the notch. Use the actual piece to make this setting, as any unevenness on the saw's top surface may cause an inaccurate measurement using just a rule or tape.

5 Start making your cuts across the piece, starting from the inside of the rabbet. Make the first cut, pull the miter gauge back, slide the piece over slightly and make the next cut. Keep repeating.

6 When you've finished your cut, you will have a good rabbet on the ends that will create the decorative offset and allow you to assemble the frame with screws.

7 Moving on to the top, mark the locations for the "handles" on the piece using the illustrations, and then get out your jigsaw. I start by making cross cuts into the board, stopping at the pencil line.

8 The next cut is a sweeping one, starting from the middle of the waste area and moving down to the bottom line, swinging to run parallel, or just shy, of the bottom line, ending at the first cut. The waste piece will then fall away.

9 I repeat these two steps for the opposite side, leaving a squared notch. For the two end cuts, a simple cross cut, followed by an intersecting rip from the end is simple work.

10 To allow the mirror to rest on all four pieces of the frame and be properly supported, a rabbet is cut along the inside edge of the two vertical sides. Start by setting the saw fence to ⅝", then adjust the blade height slightly shy of ½". Make the cut on both side pieces.

11 To clean up the rabbet, reset the saw fence to 2" and reset the blade height to ⅛". Make the cut on the two sides.

12 To make the slots for the leather straps, first use the illustration to mark the locations. Traditionally, you might use a mortiser to make these slots, but that's not a common tool in many shops. Chiseling the entire slot out sounded like too much work, so I looked around at my tools and decided my biscuit jointer would work nicely.

13 After clamping the piece tightely, I set the fence of my biscuit jointer to make the first cut starting ¼" down from the top. With the tool set to make a cut for a No. 20 biscuit, I centered the tool and plunged from first one side, and then the other.

14 I then reset the fence to cut down another ⅛" on both sides, reset the fence again, and made my final cuts. This left a decent ⅜"-wide slot.

15 To clean up the ends of the slots, I did need to use a mallet and chisel, but that was an easy task compared to clearing the whole slot by hand.

16 I screwed the frame pieces together using three brass flathead screws at each "tongue". A clamp across the pieces held everything tight during assembly.

OUTDOOR TABORET

5

In 1910, Gustav Stickley published a *Catalogue of Craftsman Furniture* that used black-and-white photos to sell his line of furniture. One of Stickley's concepts was to offer quality furniture at a price that the average man could afford. In the catalogue, the No. 602 Taboret was going for $3. That certainly seems appropriately priced for the average man. But when you stop to remember the cost of living in 1910 (take-home pay was around $15 a week), that $3 starts to feel like buying a leather sofa these days.

Happily, we can recreate Gus' round-top taboret for a minimum of expense, thereby fulfilling his dream of affordable furniture for the average man. The version I've offered here is built on the general dimensions and look of the original No. 602, but made with dimensional lumber and minimal milling. I substituted ¾"-thick legs rather than the 1½"-thick legs on the original. For my needs, I opted to build this table as an outdoor project (it fits great between the Limbert chairs on page 74), and I used pine as my wood, with a coat of paint as finish. By changing the material to oak with a stain and spray lacquer finish, this small table can be just as easily built for indoor use.

Material costs for the pine version were very low, requiring only one 1×6×8' board for the top and two 1×2×8's for the base. Total cost: Under $10.

Building for the table begins with gluing. Cross cut the 1×6 board into three lengths of around 18" in length. Arrange them side-to-side for best grain pattern and joint-match to make the square blank for the top. If your joints aren't tight, take a couple of swipes on the edges with a bench plane and test the joints again. When you have the match you want, mark the panels to maintain the order.

Because the joints are long grain-to-long grain the strength of the glue joint will be very good. However I like to use biscuits to align the pieces,

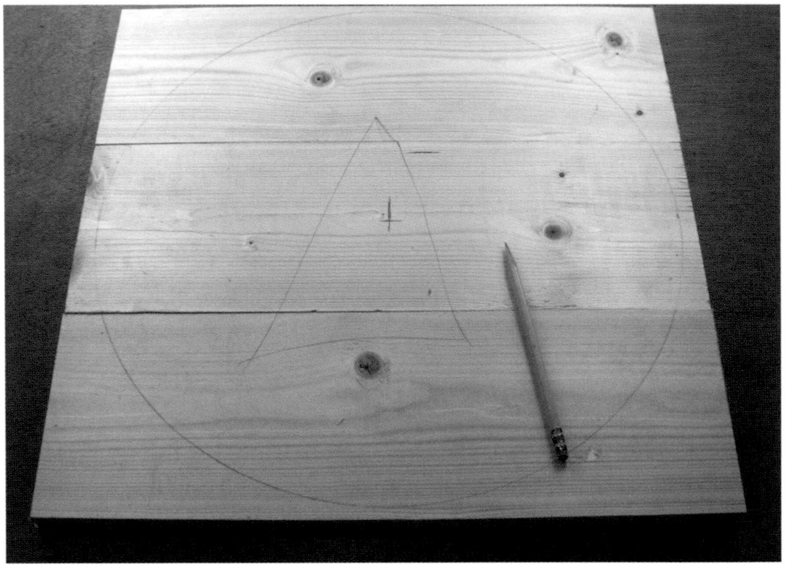

1 Start by laying out the shape of the top on your three top boards.

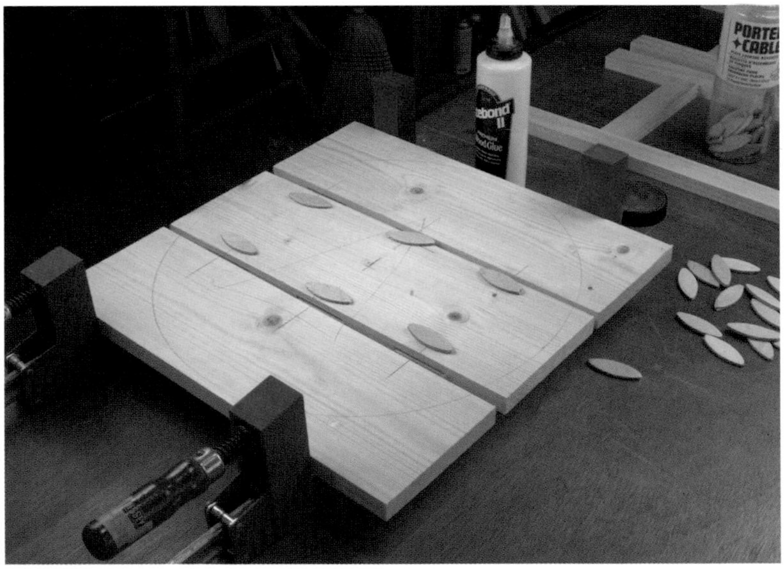

2 Mark the top for biscuit locations and cut the biscuit slots. Then glue the top together and set it aside to let the glue dry.

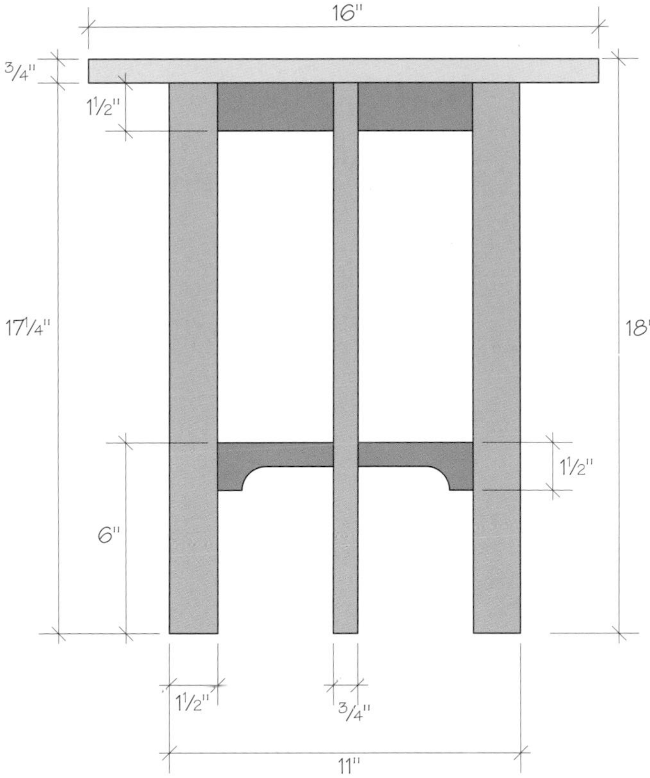

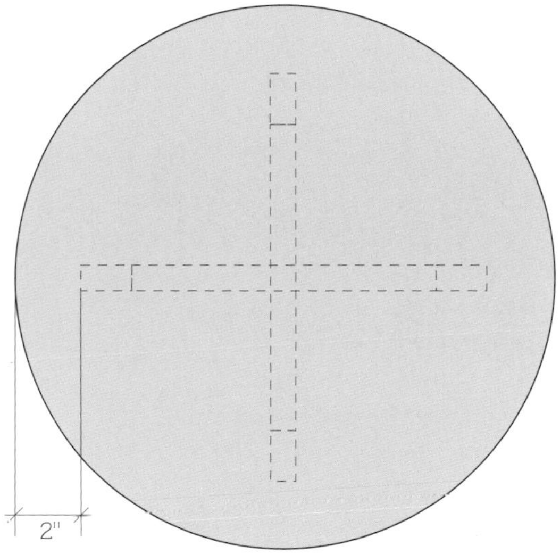

OUTDOOR TABORET • INCHES (MILLIMETERS)

REFERENCE	QUANTITY	PART	STOCK	THICKNESS	(mm)	WIDTH	(mm)	LENGTH	(mm)
A	3	top pieces	pine	3/4	19	5 1/2	140	16*	406
B	4	legs	pine	3/4	19	1 1/2	38	17 1/4	438
C	4	stretchers	pine	3/4	19	1 1/2	38	8	203

*Allow extra length for cutting to shape.

especially when there is more than one joint. Things can slip around too easily as you tighten the clamps. An uneven glue joint means extra sanding and you run the risk of adding dished sections to your top. Mark and cut the pockets to add three biscuits for each joint.

Next move to your 1×2 pieces and cut the four legs and four stretchers to length. Using a stop on your miter saw will help keep everything square and even. It doesn't take much of a difference in leg length to make a table rock.

With the pieces cut, lay them out on your work surface, layed out as the two frames will be assembled. To create the half-lap joinery on the upper and lower stretchers, you need to mark the lap locations in the center of each stretcher. The upper stretchers can be flipped over without a problem, but because of the arches cut on the lower stretchers, keeping them straight is important.

Head to your table saw (or jigsaw, if that's the tool available for this step), and cut the notches in all four stretchers. Sizing for half-lap joints come from the piece themselves. The width of the notch is the thickness of the material. The depth of the notch is half the width. Cut a little shy at first, test the fit — not too tight, and not too loose — and make any adjustments necessary.

I'd already marked the arches on the lower stretchers while marking my half-lap notches, but if you haven't done that yet, mark the two ¾"-radius curves, ¾" in

3 Cut the base pieces to length and then lay them out in position. Mark the half-lap locations on the top horizontal pieces, making sure you have a matching set.

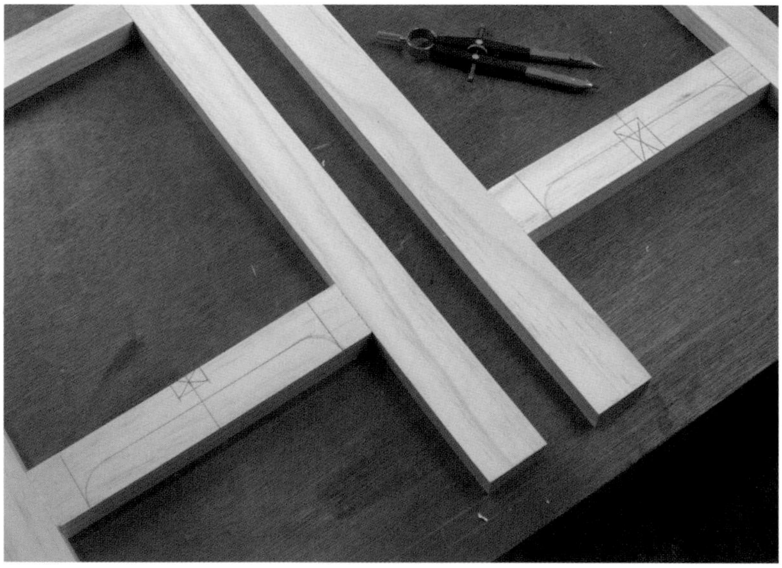

4 I also took the time to lay out the arched shapes on the lower horizontal pieces, and the corresponding half-laps on those pieces.

5 Cutting the half laps on the table saw, I first define one side of the notch...

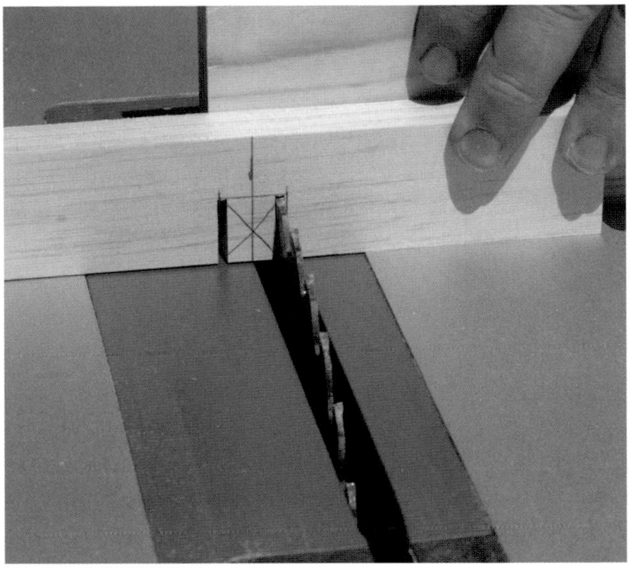

6 ...then the other side of the notch.

7 And finally just nibble away the material.

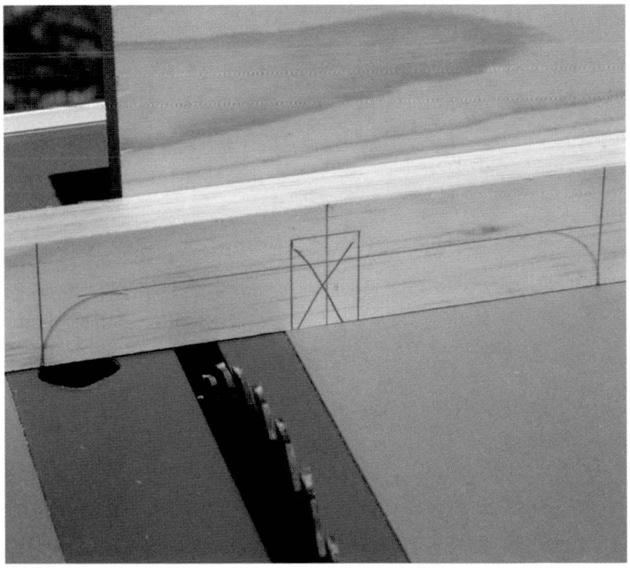

8 The half-lap on the arched stretchers require a bit more precision as there just isn't that much wood left in place. However the steps to make the notches is the same on these pieces as on the upper stretchers.

from the ends of the stretchers, and then connect the upper end of each.

This is a fairly small piece to cut with a jigsaw, and curves are a little harder. If you have access to a band saw, this would be an easy cut with that tool. In working with a jigsaw, holding the piece tightly with a clamp — even though it means stopping and starting the cuts — is much easier. Take your time and be safe.

After the cuts are made on the stretchers, take a few minutes and clean up the edges for a smoother finish. In building as many Arts & Crafts pieces as I have over the years, I've cleaned up more than one corbel. Because of this I've acquired a few smaller files and rasps. The one shown in photo 11 gets used a lot. The rounded face works great for corbels, and the flat side smooths out the transition from round-to-flat on the piece.

The next step is to assemble the base frames. To do this, I used countersunk and plugged screws through the edges of the legs and into the ends of the stretchers. Because the legs are 1½" wide, I needed to use 2½" screws to make a solid joint. I adjusted the length of my countersink bit to make sure I would properly pre-drill the hole. It's also very important the hole is drilled straight, or the screw may tear out or split the stretcher.

Start with the top stretchers, screwing them in place with one notch-up, and the other notch-down. I found this step easier to

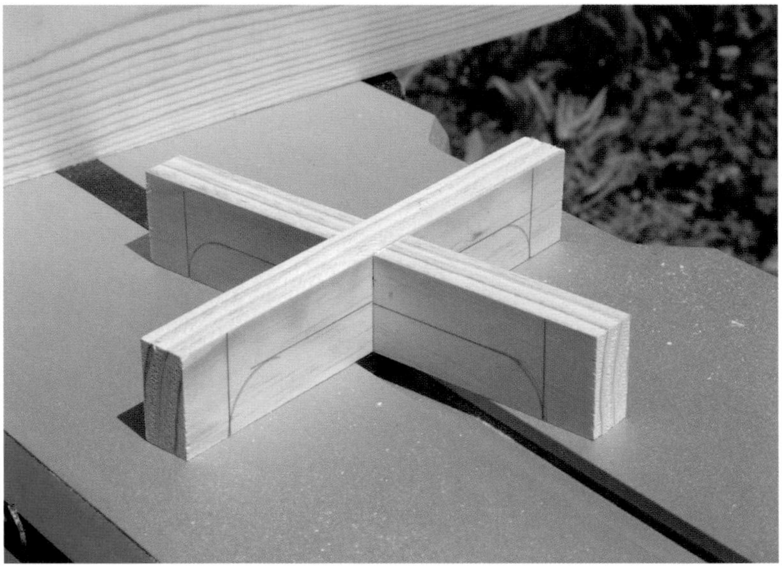

9 With the notches cut, the two stretchers fit together nicely.

10 Now all that's left on the stretchers is cutting the arches on the lower pair. A jigsaw does the job adequately, helped by clamping the piece to my work surface. If you've got a band saw handy, this step will go more quickly.

11 A little clean-up of the arches with a rasp and we're good to go.

12 The base pieces are screwed together through countersunk holes. I wanted to make this base as strong as possible, so I used a longer (2½") screw that required me to extend the pilot bit in my combination drill/countersink bit.

13 I clamped one half of the base together as I screwed the pieces in place. Note that the half-laps face each other in the center.

14 I next screwed the top stretcher in place between the two legs on the other half of the base, positioning the half lap to face up. Then I slipped the two halves together, assembling the top half-lap.

do when I used a clamp to pull the frame tight as I drove the screws home. Things stayed flush and level.

Next, press the two half-lap notches in the upper stretchers together, joining the two partial frames together at the top. To attach the lower stretchers, connect the two notches on the loose, lower stretchers and then fit the joined pieces into place on the leg frames. I oriented the notches so the joint on the lower stretchers was opposite from the joint on the upper stretchers, adding more stability to the base.

With the base near completion, take the clamps off your tabletop and mark out the 16"-diameter circle on the top. As you make your jigsaw cut to shape the circle, be careful to cut evenly and slowly to avoid blade drift that will make the edge of your top out-of-perpendicular. I recommend the "0" setting if you're using an orbital jigsaw. As always, cut slightly wide of the line to allow some space to clean up the shape. Circles are hard to get perfect with a jigsaw, so there's almost certainly going to be some clean up.

If your shop includes a band saw, you may want to use that tool to cut your circle. There are a number of jigs (both shop-made and sold commercially) that are designed just for cutting circles on the band saw. They provide an even, perpendicular cut that requires very little clean up.

But I didn't use a band saw, so there was some clean up to

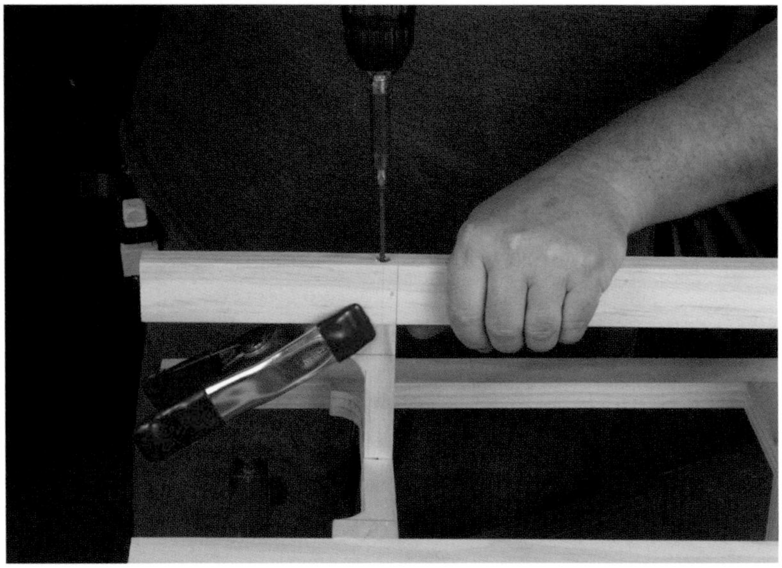

15 Lastly, I made a mark 5½" up from the bottom of the leg, pre-drilled and then ssembled the lower half lap and screwed the final stretcher in place.

16 Take the clamps off your top and sand down any excess glue squeeze-out. Then take your jigsaw and cut the top to shape.

17 I sanded the top to make the joints flat, then used my trim router and a radius bit to round-over both edges of the top.

18 The top is attached to the base using two screws, up through the one stretcher. The importance here is to have the grain of the top running in parallel with the stretcher used to attach the top. This will avoid any problems with wood movement due to changes in humidity.

achieve a reasonably round, even top. Some more time with a rasp and some 80-grit sandpaper smoothed the edge and made the top ready for the next step.

To make the top more user-friendly, and to protect the edge from splitting when exposed to sun and weather on the porch, I added a ¼" roundover to the top and bottom edges of the top.

As this piece was made of pine, I want to share a cautionary tale with you. I added a coat of paint to the table and top before I'd fastened the top to the base, and set it outside — to admire it, of course. The next morning my top was shaped like a taco shell. Pine will adjust dramatically to changes in humidity. If you have the time, it would make sense to let the boards for your top acclimate to the conditions (inside or out) where the table will eventually live. My taco-top wasn't a loss, though. I flipped it over and let it sit for another day or two, and as you can see in the opening photo, equilibrium was achieved.

Two clearance holes through one of the top stretchers allowed me to attach the top to the base with screws. I oriented the top with the grain running parallel to the stretcher that I put the attaching screws through, avoiding concerns of wood movement.

A couple of coats of an exterior-grade paint and the project was done.

Simon
Schama
POWER OF ART
STUDIO FURNITURE

PINE BOOKCASE

6

About ten years ago I was given a set of old house windows. Pine frame, diamond-patterned mullions, in decent shape. They sat in my garage for a while until one weekend I was feeling creative and decided they'd make nice doors on a glass-front bookcase.

While my creativity was cranking, my bank account was a little skinny. I'd also decided I was going to finish the bookcase that weekend. Off to the home center store. The result is essentially what you see here, minus the doors. An attractive, easy-to-assemble pine bookcase. The doors were a nice touch, but I think the case works just as it is.

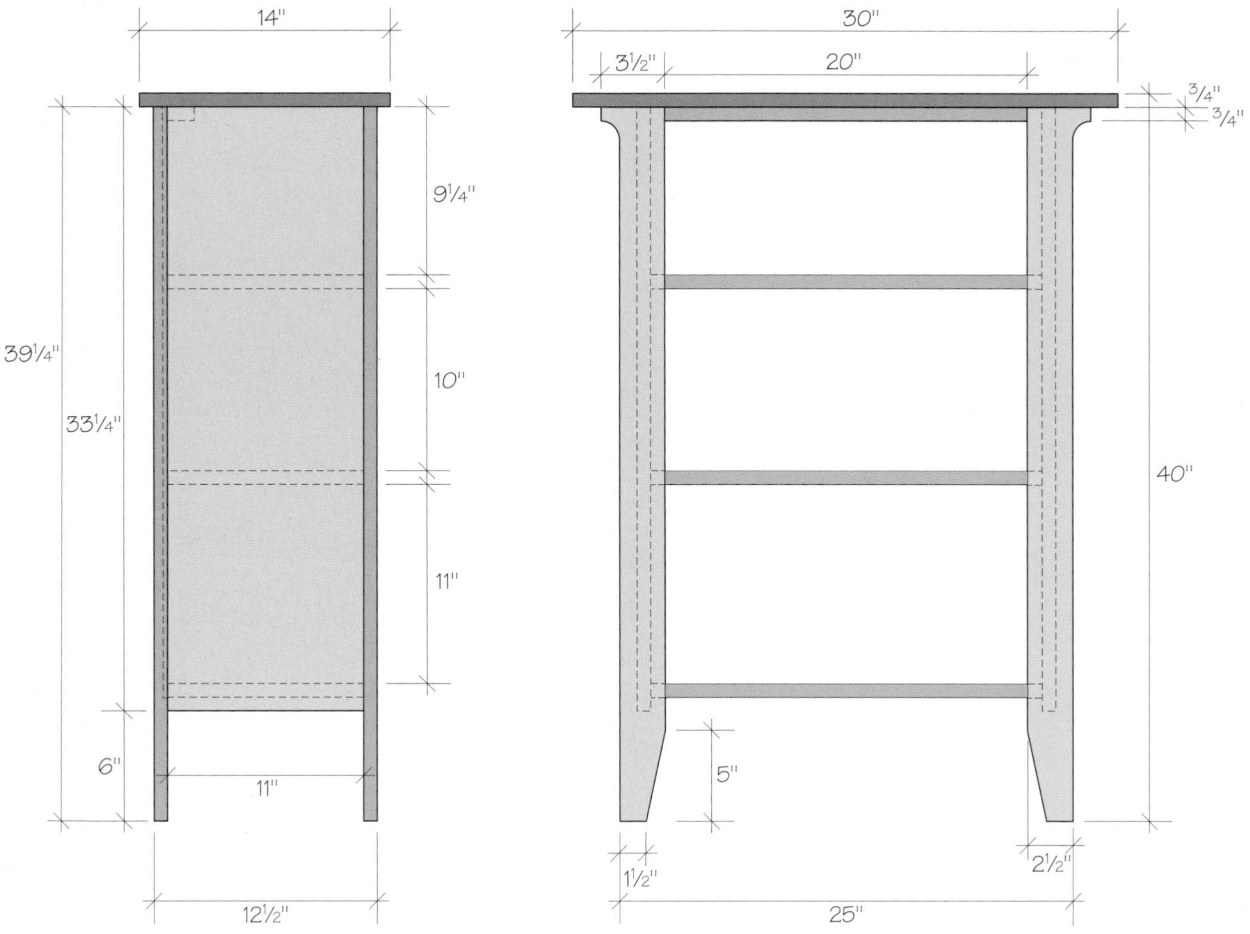

PINE BOOKCASE • INCHES (MILLIMETERS)

REFERENCE	QUANTITY	PART	STOCK	THICKNESS	(mm)	WIDTH	(mm)	LENGTH	(mm)
A	1	top	pine	3/4	19	14	356	30	762
B	2	sides	pine	3/4	19	11	279	33 1/4	845
C	4	legs	pine	3/4	19	3 1/2	89	39 1/4	997
D	3	shelves	pine	3/4	19	11	279	21 1/2	546
E	1	back rail	pine	3/4	19	1 1/2	38	21 1/2	546
F	1	back	plywd	1/4	6	21 1/4	540	32 1/2	826

1 Pocket screws are perfect for this project. I cut pockets in the underside of each of the three shelves.

2 I held the bottom shelf up ¾" from the bottom edge of each side and screwed it in place.

One of the hardest parts of this project was getting decent pine. Or rather, straight pine. Cheap was my watchword, so as I was standing in the aisle at Lowe's, I knew basic pine was what I wanted. Select pine was staged right next to it, and the knot-free, straight lengths were calling to me. I checked price and saw that the select pine was three times as much. Poplar? Right up there with the select pine. So I picked through the cheaper boards to find the best.

After carefully matching the boards for best edges (for glue-up) and for grain match, I glued the panels for the top, the shelves and for the two sides. The shelves and two sides are sized to finish at 11" wide, which is two 1×6s glued together. The top was two 1×8s that were then ripped to finish width.

PUTTING IT TOGETHER

Construction was pretty straightforward. After cutting the finished panels to length I used pocket screws to attach the three shelves between the two sides. I held the bottom shelf up ¾" to avoid chances of splitting in the bottom of the soft pine sides. The spacing for the other two shelves is provided in the illustration, but feel free to adjust for your needs.

The legs themselves are actually big corbels, and the only real touch of design on the case. The curved top and tapered foot are the first things to which the eyes are drawn, so getting them right is important. I wanted to keep the outside edge of each leg as straight and clean as possible. One option would have been a ¼" hardboard template and a router. Another would have been to cut the leg and the corbel curve with my jigsaw. Instead, I went for a combination move, using my bench top table saw to cut up the length of the leg (ripping at 2½" inches), and stopping the cut just before the start of the curve at the top of the leg.

This step isn't dangerous at all, but it does require planning and attention. A mark added to your table saw fence will show you where the blade starts cutting wood. This is your stopping point. When you reach that point with your leg, hold the piece in position and carefully turn the saw off. Wait until the blade stops spinning and then lift the leg off the blade. Don't try and lift the leg with the blade spinning, it's asking for a dangerous kick-back.

Rip all four legs up to the beginning of the curve, then head for your jigsaw to complete the curve cut and the bevel at the foot.

HOLDING THE BACK

I used a ¼"-thick plywood back for the case. To keep it simple, I routed a ¼" × ⅜" rabbet along the inside edge of each back leg, stopping the rabbet 5" up from the bottom of each leg.

After some finish sanding to most of the interior surfaces, I attached the back and front legs

3 The two upper shelves can be spaced to fit your book needs and then screwed in place.

4 Cut a clean rip up the legs, but stop at the beginning of the curve. I use a mark on my table saw fence to show the initial contact point of the blade.

5 A jigsaw is used to finish up the cut to create the corbel.

6 My waste piece is square here because the curve was cut away using smaller cuts to keep the blade from binding in the curve. This is a fragile piece, so use care.

7 A simple bevel cut on the inside of each foot adds an extra bit of flair.

8 A rabbet cut on the inside edge of each back leg allows the back to be slid into place.

using trim nails. Screws seemed overkill for this task, and a little glue along the joint added extra strength. Don't used too much glue, or the squeeze-out will keep you cleaning things up longer than you want.

When I attached the back legs, I used the back itself to help space the legs. It allowed a ¾" overhang of the legs to the interior of the case. Just right.

The back slips into place between the back legs and the case itself. Leave it loose for now to make finishing easier. Eventually it will be nailed in place to the lower shelf and to the final piece of wood: the back rail. This is simply a strip nailed in place between the sides to add a little stability and give us a place to attach the back.

The top is attached to the case by putting two screws up through the back rail, and then adding two pieces of L-shaped hardware to attach to the sides.

A final sanding for everything and you can add a finish. I like the look of the knots and other subtle imperfections in the wood so wanted to stain the piece. I used Minwax Chestnut stain and top coated the piece with brush-on lacquer. Though it takes slightly longer to dry, it's easier to apply finish to a piece this large with a brush (and cheaper!).

9 With a clamp keeping everything in place, the back rail is simply nailed in place between the two sides.

10 I used 2" trim nails to hold the back legs in place, using the loose back to help locate the legs.

11 The front legs are attached the same way, and then recessed using a nail set.

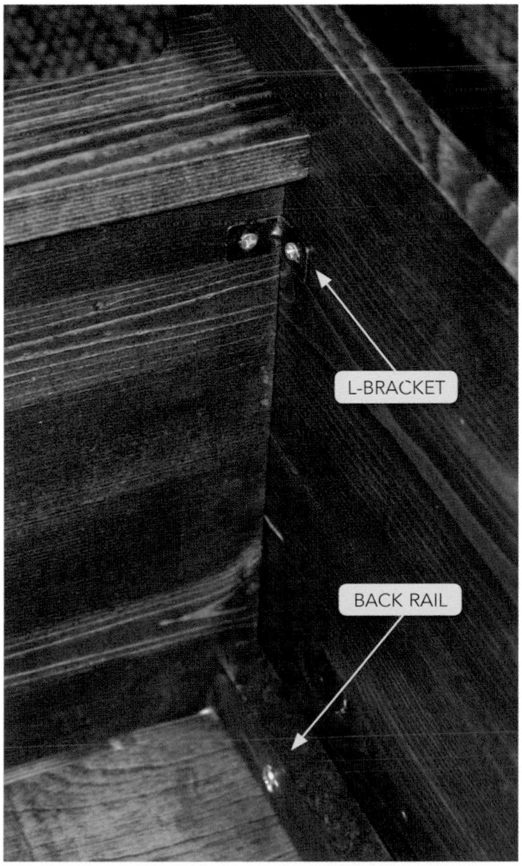

12 The top is screwed in place with L-shaped brackets at the front of the case (between the side and top) and up through the back rail at the rear of the case.

My Books Don't Fit!

One of the things I love about this project is it's adaptability. The height and width of the bookcase are purely arbitrary. The depth works well with the material sizes available from the home center stores, but the case could easily be another foot taller, or shorter. As for width, it can certainly get thinner, but I wouldn't push much past 30"-wide without adding some extra support under the shelves. Otherwise your books will add a sag to the center of the shelf.
You can add extra support to the shelves by simply gluing a ¾" x 1"-wide piece of pine on edge to the underside of the shelf's front edge. Even with this upgrade, I'd be hesitant to go past 36"-wide without adding a center support of some type. But don't hesitate to adjust your case to fit your needs!

EVOLUTION
A MOVEMENT
ARTS & CRAFTS IN
AUSTRALIA

OUTDOOR TABLE

7

This outdoor trestle dining table is a fairly straightforward trestle design that is seen in a variety of Arts & Crafts pieces. Designed to seat four, the dimensions could be extended slightly to accommodate six. All that would be required would be to extend the length of the lower stretchers and add another stretcher at the top for stability. The top would need to be lengthened by about 20", but other than that, the option is there.

As this is an outdoor piece, I've used pine for construction, but the piece could be built from oak and finished with an indoor stain and top coat. For more formal use, the top slats could be replaced with a piece of oak veneer plywood, also available at your home center store.

There are a lot of pieces to this project, so it's best to think of it in two main sections: the base and the top. The base itself is made up of three parts; the two legs and the stretcher that runs between the legs. And just to make things interesting, the legs are actually built in halves and then glued together to add mass and stability to the whole base.

THE LEGS & STRETCHER

Construction starts with marking the corner notch cuts necessary on the four tops (supports) and four bottoms (bracket feet) of the legs. The cuts are identical and can all be made at the same time.

The four bracket feet also have an arch cut in the lower edge that is made with a jigsaw.

With the bracket and support cuts made, the stretcher that provides stability to the lower portion of the base is screwed together.

One of the tricks with this table was hiding as much of the joinery as possible. Because of this, the legs are screwed to the stretcher and bracket halves from the inside, creating two half-assemblies that are then biscuited and glued together.

The inner brackets are first screwed to the stretcher, then

1 Mark the location of the corner bevels on the four upper supports and the four base pieces, and also mark the lower "arch" on the base pieces.

2 I used my miter saw as the most efficient tool to cut the bevels on the corners of the eight pieces, but this could also be easily accomplished with a jigsaw.

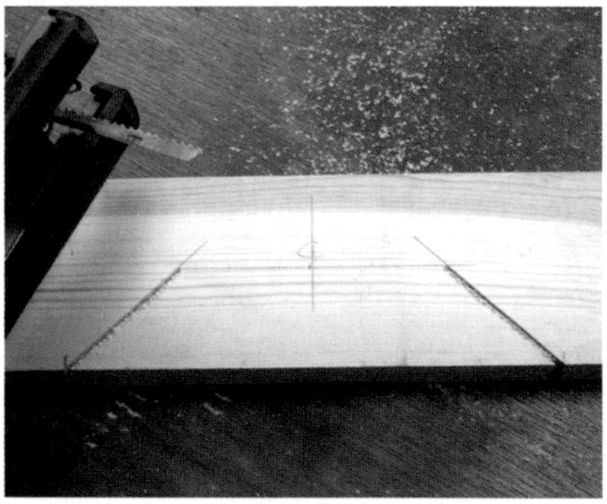

3 I did use my jigsaw to first define both sides of the lower arches.

4 I next cut a sweeping curve from the center of the arch to one of the corners, allowing the waste piece to drop free. I then cut from the open space along the top edge of the arch to the other corner. Both waste pieces are shown here, with only a little trimming at the top of the arch to finish the cut.

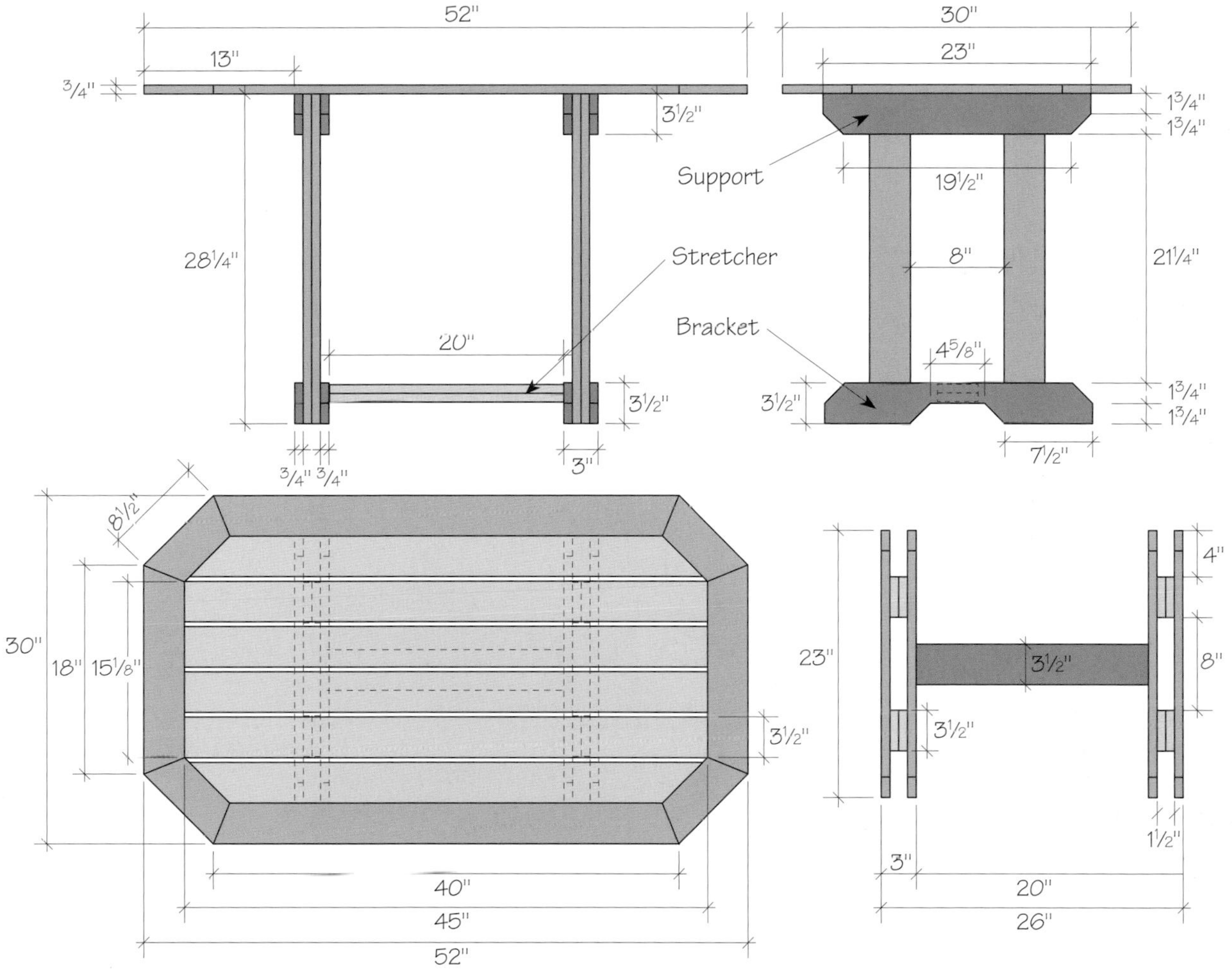

OUTDOOR TABLE • INCHES (MILLIMETERS)

REFERENCE	QUANTITY	PART	STOCK	THICKNESS	(mm)	WIDTH	(mm)	LENGTH	(mm)
A	8	legs	pine	3/4	19	3 1/2	89	28 1/4	718
B	8	supports/brackets	pine	3/4	19	3 1/2	89	23	584
C	2	stretchers	pine	3/4	19	3 1/2	89	20	508
D	2	top frame	pine	3/4	19	3 1/2	89	40	1016
E	2	top frame	pine	3/4	19	3 1/2	89	8 1/2	216
F	2	top frame	pine	3/4	19	3 1/2	89	18	457
G	6	top slats	pine	3/4	19	3 1/2	89	45	1143

the legs are screwed in place on the brackets. The inner supports are then screwed in place against the legs.

The outer half of the leg assemblies are screwed together separately and then the two halves are glued together to form the completed legs. The biscuits are used to align the two halves of the leg posts to keep things straight and to reduce sanding and clean-up work of sloppy joints.

THE TOP

The top was also a little interesting in that I didn't want to add a rabbet ledge to the frame to support the top slats. Trying to figure a way to keep things level and at a ¾" thickness was interesting, but ultimately not too hard. The top consists of a ¾"-thick eight-sided frame that is biscuited together at the joints. This required both 45° and 22.5° miter cuts. I was able to use my miter saw, but if that tool isn't available to you, a circular saw and a good protractor will do.

The frame itself is inadequate to provide enough support for the top, so I designed it with the first slat in from either side glued and biscuited to the long frame edge and the two frame corner pieces. This provides a solid support to the frame. The middle section is then glued in place between the two rigid outside lengths, and then the top is screwed to the upper supports on the table legs, holding everything in place. I plugged the four holes in the top slats and sand-

5 The center beam or stretcher is made of two pieces of 3½"-wide material glued and screwed together from the underside. Since this piece is painted and this is the underside, I didn't bother to countersink the screws.

6 On the inner feet brackets, I marked the approximate location of where the lower beam would intersect the bracket. I started to mark and drill for only two screws, but decided there was enough room for four.

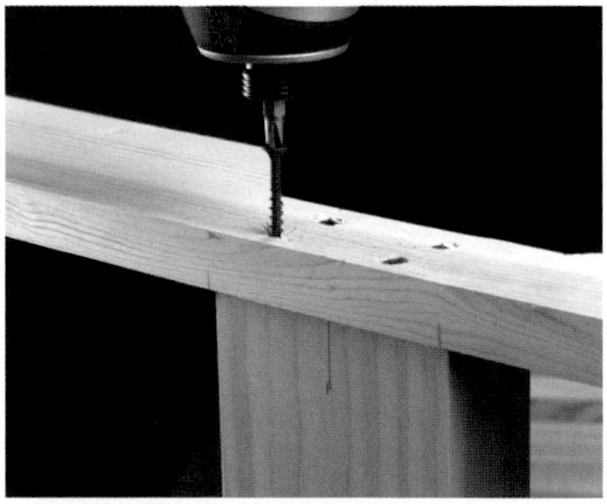

7 I used 2½"-long screws to attach the inner bracket feet. I didn't countersink or plug these holes on my table, but were I to do it over, I think I'd take that step the second time around, as these were the only visible (but fairly well hidden) screws when the table was complete.

8 I then set the base frame on my work surface and made sure it was sitting flat before screwing the second inner bracket foot in place.

9 Moving on to the posts for the legs, I marked biscuit locations for six biscuits (three per edge) along the post-piece edges. I found it easier to make this cut with two of the pieces held together to provide more bearing surface during the cut.

10 I next moved back to the bracket foot assembly and marked perpendicular lines on the feet to indicate the post locations. By the way, I love my Veritas Sliding Square for this type of work (www.leevalley.com).

11 Starting with one end, I screwed one post in place with four screws, then put only one screw in the second post.

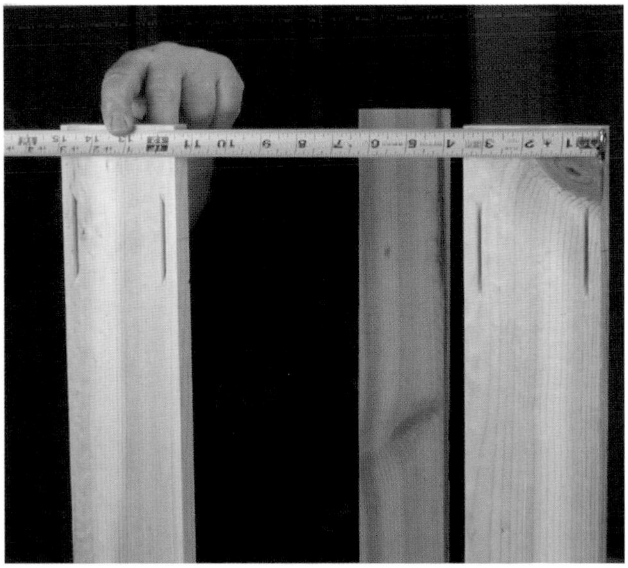

12 I measured across the two posts down by the feet, and then made sure that the dimension was the same at the top of the posts, then put the last three screws in the bottom of that post.

ing everything smooth, adding a roundover profile to the upper and lower edges of the top.

A couple of coats of a flat exterior-grade paint finished the table up, and it was ready for the party.

In my case, I wanted to add a standard table umbrella. I did this easily enough by screwing a 3½" × 3½" square plate to the underside of the top slats, dead center on the table. A hole saw sized to fit my umbrella made the hole through the top easily. I then inserted the umbrella, squared the pole to the tabletop, and marked the location on the lower stretcher. Another minute with the hole saw and a second hole was cut through the lower stretcher.

These two holes stabilized the umbrella adequately, but if you want to avoid the umbrella turning in a breeze, a simple screw through the side of the lower stretcher and into the umbrella pole will do the trick.

13 I then screwed the top supports in place at the top of the posts. Both sets of posts and the inner supports are shown here.

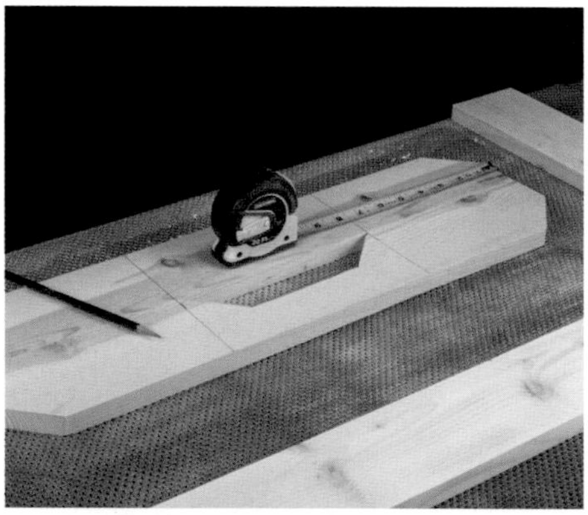

14 Moving to the outer halves of the posts/feet/supports, I first marked the post locations on the remaining upper supports and bracket feet, making sure the lines were perpendicular to the bottom of the feet brackets.

15 I then screws the second half of the posts to the top supports only, again checking squareness as I moved forward.

16 To double check the alignment, I put a couple of biscuits (without glue) in place in each half of the posts and pushed the two halves together. I then marked the post location on the outer bracket feet.

17 After disassembling the post halves, I finished screwing the posts to the outer bracket feet from the inside face of the post halves.

18 The assembled outer leg sections were then glued in place with the biscuits all in their slots for proper alignment. They really do make things easier during a large glue-up.

19 Work on a flat surface to make sure the feet brackets rest evenly on the surface. Depending on the number of clamps you have available, you may need to do one side, and then the other.

20 I made a squareness guide on my work surface to help me lay out and cut all the miters for the top pieces. Start with the squared corner, then work around the outside of the frame, finally filling in the center slats.

21 Assembly starts with one long frame piece and the adjoining two corner pieces. Fit the first slat into that space once the frame is established, then mark and cut for biscuits.

22 Glue and clamp these piece together following this same pattern (outside frame first, first slat, then corners) to assemble the one side of the frame. Then repeat this process for the opposite side of the top frame.

23 Mark the biscuit locations for the four middle slats on the two short frame pieces, but don't glue this up yet.

24 When the outer frame sections are dry, mark the biscuit locations joining the outer sections and the short frame pieces.

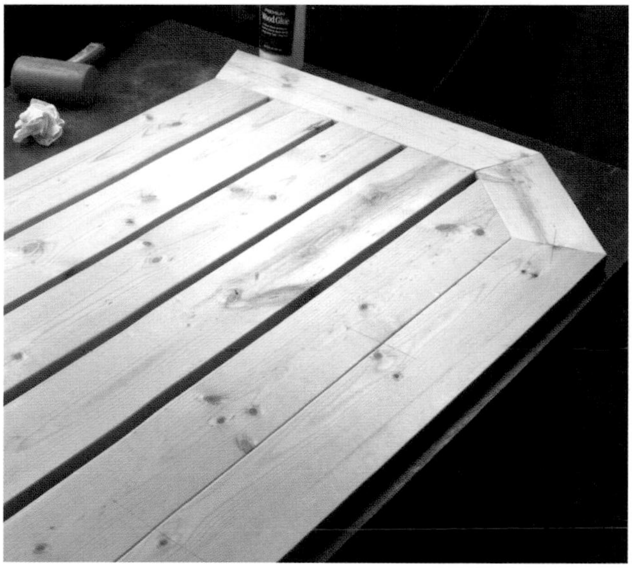

25 Start assembling the top by gluing one outer frame section to the middle section.

26 Then add the other outer frame section, tapping and clamping the frame into place to adjust all the joints as you go. Clamp it tight and let it dry.

MANTEL CLOCK

8

Clocks are a great staple in the Arts & Crafts catalogs. Honestly, there are a lot more clocks, mantel, or otherwise, available by today's craftsmen than were ever available during the original Arts & Crafts movement. It's also my opinion that the clocks of today are a lot better looking. Good for us!

This mantel clock is very simple, and takes very little material, much of which is likely available in your scrap pile. If not, go build the hall bench and then you'll have the necessary materials for the clock, too.

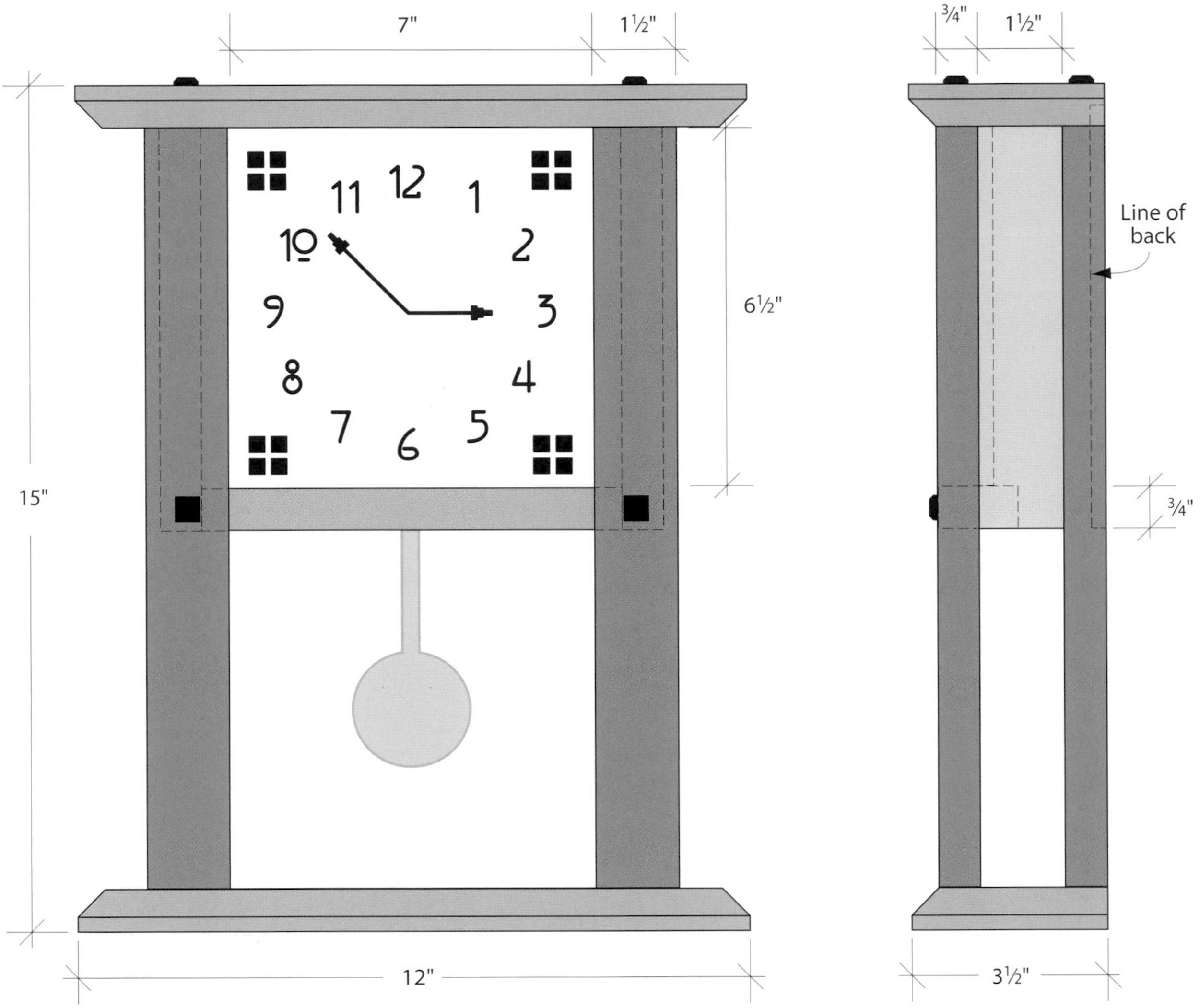

MANTEL CLOCK • INCHES (MILLIMETERS)

REFERENCE	QUANTITY	PART	STOCK	THICKNESS	(mm)	WIDTH	(mm)	LENGTH	(mm)
A	4	posts	oak	3/4	19	1 1/2	38	13 1/2	343
B	2	top/bottom	oak	3/4	19	3 1/2	89	12	305
C	2	sides	oak	3/4	19	1 1/2	38	7 1/4	184
D	1	center rail	oak	3/4	19	1 1/2	38	8	203
E	1	face	oak	1/4	6	8	203	6 1/2	165
F	1	back*	plywd	1/4	6	7 1/2	191	7 1/2	191

* Cut to fit.

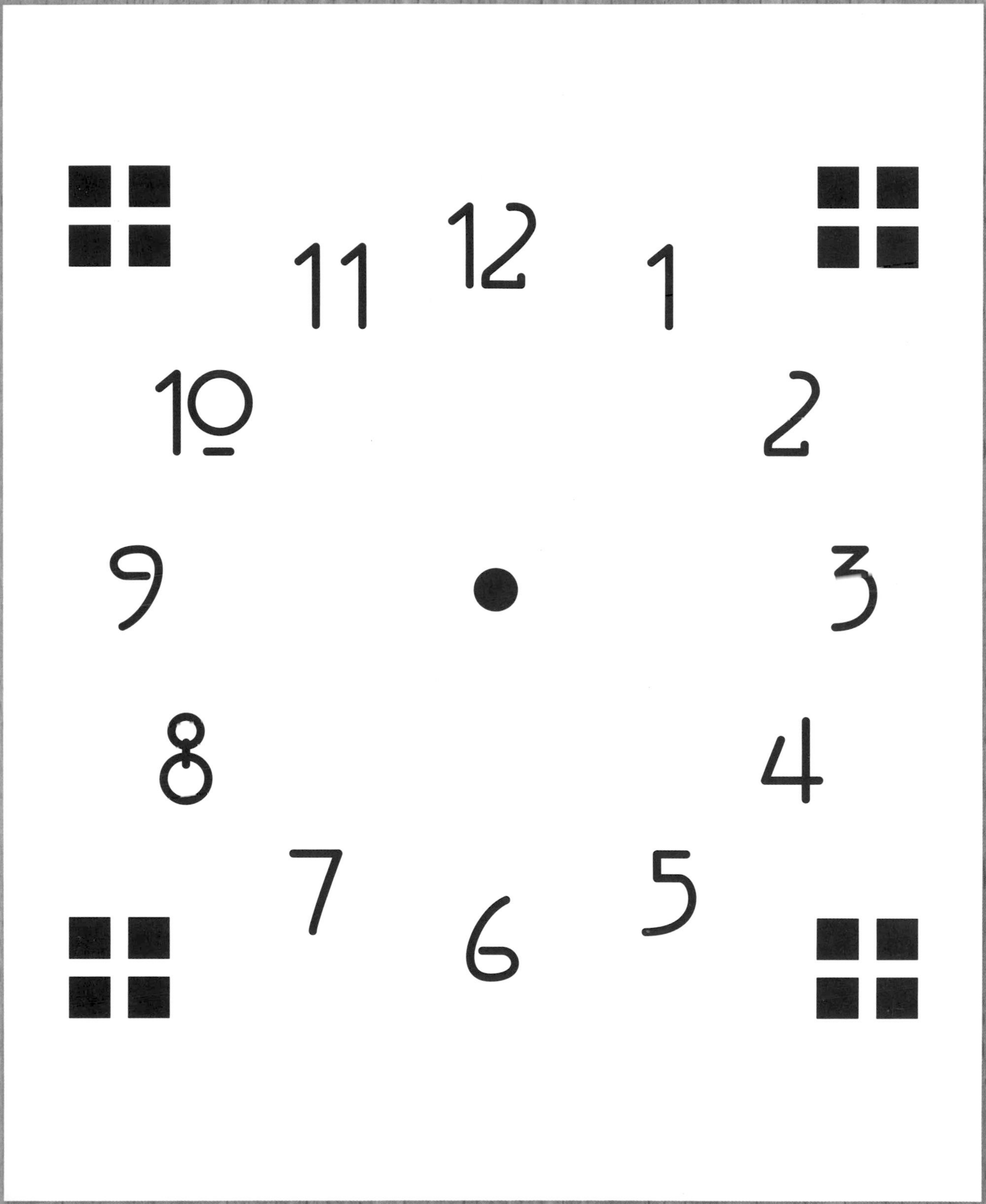
12
11
1
10
2
9
3
8
4
7
5
6

This clock is pretty straightforward to construct, but with a few little steps to make things interesting. I'm using a stock quartz clock movement and pendulum set from Rockler.com (item #28571, $14.29) and sword clock hands, also from Rockler (item #36848, $2.79). I know these mechanicals work for the clock, but there are likely many other similar sets that will also fit comfortably.

I started by cutting all the oak pieces to length. You can lay out the clock almost how it will look after this first step. That leads us to the first piece of fitting.

The center rail is mostly decorative, to frame the face of the clock. But to assemble the clock and keep the center rail out of the way of the swinging pendulum, the rail needs to be set flush to the front of the posts. That means we need to notch the rail around the posts. I marked a ¾"-deep × ½"-wide notch on each side of the center rail. I used a flush-cutting hand saw to carefully cut the notches, but you could also do it with a band saw, or jigsaw if necessary. Just not as clean a cut.

The next step is to attach the sides between the front and back posts. This is a long grain-to-long grain glue joint and as such doesn't require biscuits for strength. However, because the sides are set in ¼" from the outsides of the posts, I wanted to use biscuits to help align things.

Using No. 10 biscuits, I cut slots on both sides of the side pieces. I reset the fence on the biscuit jointer to allow the ¼" off-

1 After cutting the pieces to length, I marked the center rail for the necessary notches.

2 A fine-tooth hand saw cuts the notches quickly and cleanly. First a cut from the top...

3 ...then another from the side...

4 ...and the notch piece is free.

5 A piece of scrap from one of the posts shows how the notch interacts with the clock frame.

6 The notch slips behind the front post and the sides will fit tight up against the end of the center rail once in place. Check the side location, and mark it on the post.

set, then cut the slots in the front and back posts on both sides.

I added glue to the biscuits and sides and glued both together, using a clamp to pull things up tight.

While the sides were drying, I used my trim router and a bearing-guided chamfer bit to add a ⅜" × ⅜" chamfer to the top and bottom pieces.

When the sides were dry, I did a little sanding on them, close to finish, then got ready to attach the center rail. The rail is mounted 6¾" down from the top edge of each side assembly. I wanted the rail to attach solidly to the sides, so I drilled angled holes through the back of the center rail, stopping just short of entering the front posts. I then countersunk the hole and use a 1¼" long flathead screw to attach the center rail.

A little sanding on the top and bottom pieces and I was ready to screw the bottom in place.

The clock face is cut from ¼"-thick plywood. Use the clock frame itself to fit the face. It should fit snugly between the two sides, and it should fit tightly against the center rail and flush to the tops of the posts. When you have it sized correctly, mark the face opening on the face piece, then mark an × to determine the center of the face. Follow the directions on the clock mechanism, and the photos here to attach the clock mechanism to the clock.

I've provided a full-size clock face here on page 65. Copy or

7 The sides are held between the posts, using biscuits. The side is actually recessed ¼" back between the posts, but I've got it propped flush to mark the biscuit locations.

8 Slots are cut centered on both sides of the side pieces.

9 The posts receive slots offset by ¼". I set two posts together to give more surface for the biscuit jointer while making the cuts.

10 The pieces all glued up and ready to go. Try not to use too much glue, or you'll just end up cleaning it off.

11 A clamp or two across the side keeps the joints tight while the glue dries.

12 For a nice detail I added a ⅜" × ⅜" chamfer along the front and both sides of the top and bottom.

13 A carefully placed (and angled) screw attaches the center rail to the sides of the clock.

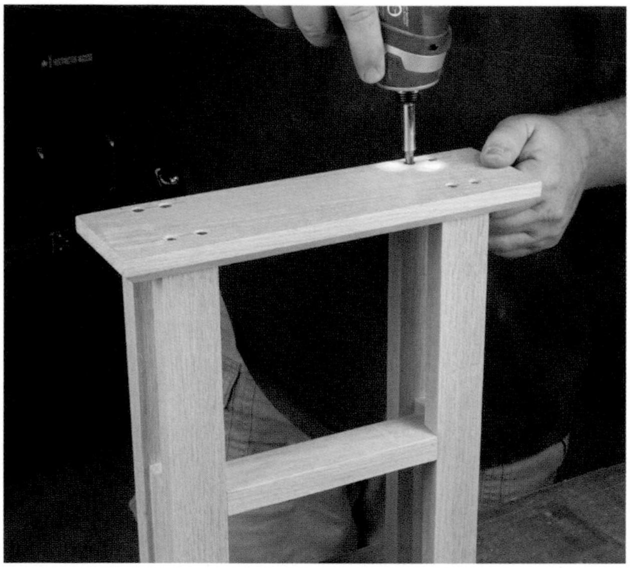

14 The bottom is held in place with two countersunk screws per post.

15 Cut the ¼" face to fit in the clock opening. Mark the opening location, then connect the corners on the face to determine the center of the clock face. Drill a hole sized to allow the clock mechanism to poke through the front.

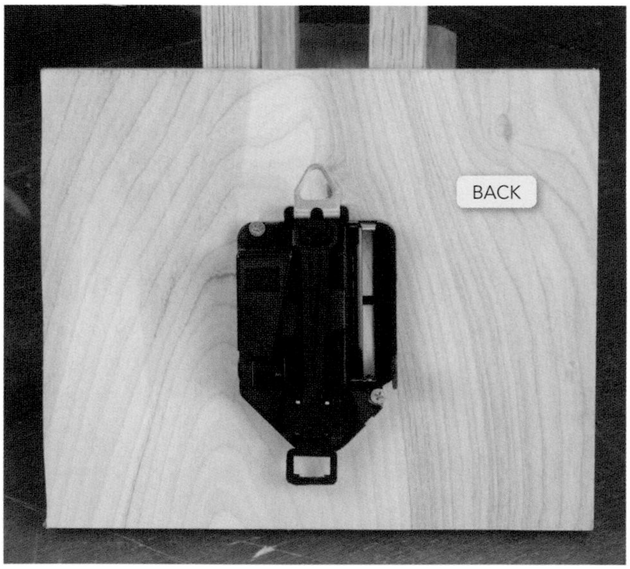

16 The mechanism is attached to the clock face with two screws. Use a hand screwdriver to avoid over-tightening the screws.

17 Just to make sure everything was working right, I installed the clock mechanism to the front and tried it in place.

18 I also took this opportunity to shorten the rod for the pendulum to a length that fit well with the opening.

print the face on whatever bond paper appeals to your tastes. To prepare my paper face, I sprayed a couple of coats of flat lacquer directly to the printed face. As there is no glass on this clock, the lacquer will help protect the face.

Once the face is ready, drill a hole in the center and carefully attach the paper face to the clock face using a craft spray adhesive (3M Super 77 Spray Adhesive).

Attach the clock mechanism and make any adjustments to the pendulum.

Position the top in place on the posts, then put one screw in the center of each post. I pre-drilled a hole at each location, then countersunk the head. These screws are then hidden under a black plastic cap designed to look like a square ebony plug. I used a rabbeting bit in my trim router to cut a rabbet in the top piece and the two rear posts, to fit my ¼"-thick plywood back. Fit the back to the rabbet and screw in place.

I then attached the clock face to the inside of the post/sides, reattached the clock mechanism, and added the back. Not a bad afternoon's work!

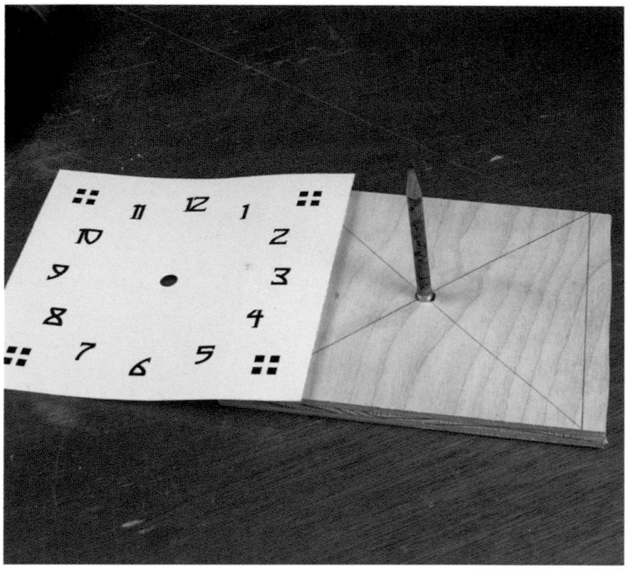

19 Once the spray adhesive is on, use a pencil to help align the paper face to the clock face.

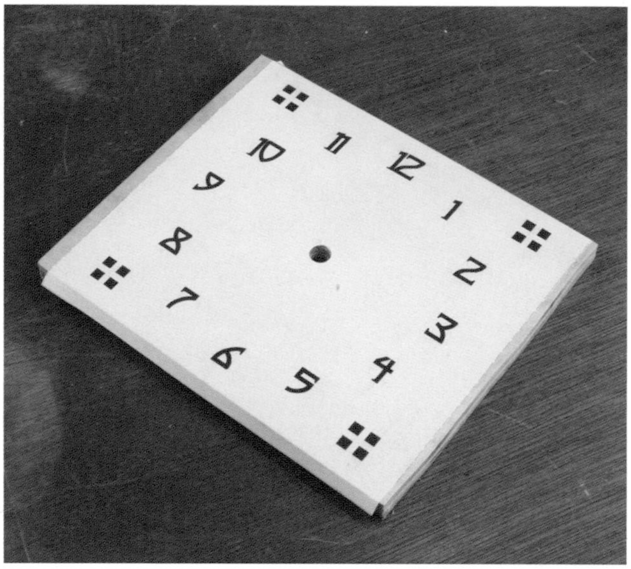

20 Because the clock face's top and bottom edge only butt against the center rail and the underside of the top, I left extra length on the pattern so it can be tucked-over, providing extra tension.

21 The product shown here (Artisan Accents from www.fastcap.com) is essentially a mortising chisel used to create a patterned depression in the wood that simple black plastic caps are glued into. Who needs ebony?

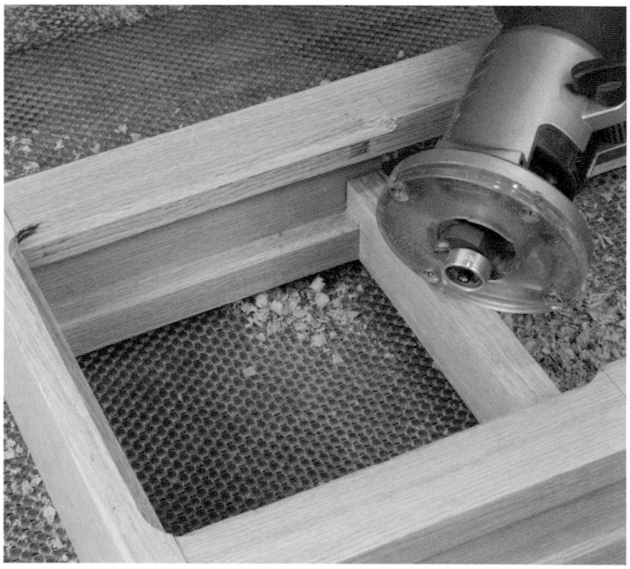

22 The ¼" back fits into a ¼" x ¼" rabbet cut into the top and back posts.

23 Rather than square off the corners of the rabbet, I sanded the back corners to fit. Four ½" flathead screws will secure the back to the posts.

24 I stained the clock (disassembled) with Minwax Antique Oak gel stain. A couple of coats of a semi-gloss spray lacquer (no more than two cans....) tops off the piece.

25 After removing the exposed screws in the top, the face piece is screwed in place, and the top is then reattached.

26 Not all of Greene & Greene's plugs actually hid any joinery, so why not add a little design and function! I added two more plugs (hiding nothing) at the junctions of the cross rail and the front posts. With the "ebony" plugs glued in place with a dab of SuperGlue, add the hands and the clock is ready for the mantel.

LIMBERT CHAIR

9

I love the outdoors. And I'm impressed with whatever forces in the universe have made it possible for me to purchase a collapsible canvas-and-metal camp chair for under $20. But when you're looking for furniture for a more permanent outdoor setting, then you need something special. This chair design caught my eye in a book called *Arts & Crafts Furniture*, by Kevin Rodel and Jonathan Binzen.

Actually there were two chairs similar in design. A nearly-black painted version by Scottish designer Charles Rennie Mackintosh that, it appears, influenced American designer Charles Limbert who created a wood-finished cafe chair. I liked the look of both chairs, and quickly recognized that they would easily adapt to our "minimal" approach to construction. My version here is an amalgam of the two, but because of my use of corbels under the arms, I'm going to give Charles Limbert the stronger claim.

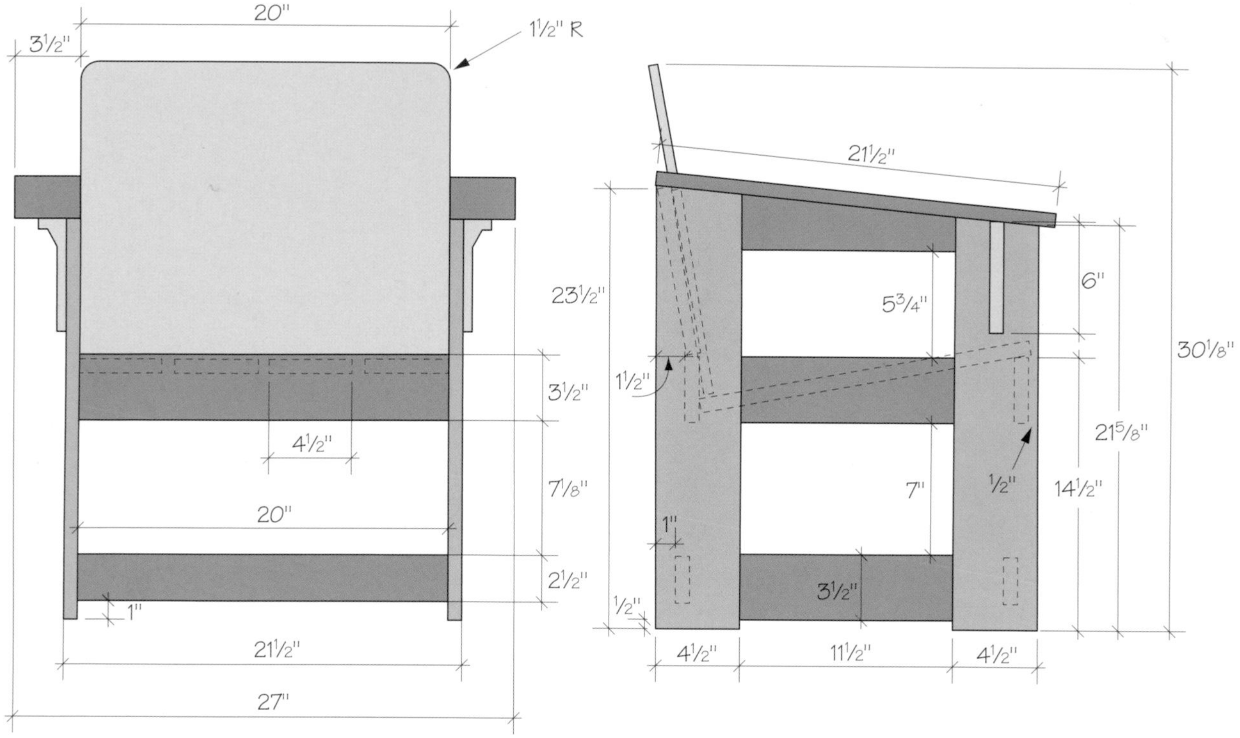

LIMBERT CHAIR • INCHES (MILLIMETERS)

REFERENCE	QUANTITY	PART	STOCK	THICKNESS	(mm)	WIDTH	(mm)	LENGTH	(mm)
A	2	front legs*	poplar	3/4	19	4 1/2	115	22	559
B	2	back legs*	poplar	3/4	19	4 1/2	115	24	610
C	6	side stretchers	poplar	3/4	19	3 1/2	89	11 1/2	292
D	2	f&b stretchers	poplar	3/4	19	3 1/2	89	20	508
E	2	f&b stretchers	poplar	3/4	19	2 1/2	64	20	508
F	2	arms	poplar	3/4	19	3 1/2	89	21 1/2	546
G	4	seat slats	poplar	3/4	19	4 1/2	115	18	457
H	2	corbels	poplar	3/4	19	1 1/2	38	6	152
J	1	back	plywd	5/8	16	20	508	18	457
K	4	cleats**	poplar	3/4	19	3/4	19	9	229

* Allows length for miter cut on one end.

** Cut to fit.

1 The two sides are simple frames, though I did go the extra effort to make the vertical pieces thinner ($4\frac{1}{2}$"-wide) to provide more appealing proportions. Lay out the sides pieces to mark for pocket screws, making sure that you have both a left and right side.

2 My pocket screw jig makes quick work of the holes drilled in only the horizontal parts.

As my version was destined for use outside, I changed a lower shelf on the Limbert chair, to two stretchers at the front and back. This along with a seat made of slats, an angled seat and spacing for drainage all make this a more outdoor-friendly chair. I borrowed Mackintosh's painted finish, however, to help in weatherproofing the chair.

PLY AND POPLAR

My materials consisted of 1×3, 1×4 and 1×6 poplar boards, and a small piece of $\frac{5}{8}$"-thick birch plywood. In drawing up the chair, I tried to use $5\frac{1}{2}$"-wide boards for the legs and was disappointed with the final look. After some mental debate, I opted to rip the 1×6 boards for the legs to $4\frac{1}{2}$" for a better look. If you're without a table saw, a jigsaw and a plane to clean up the edges will do in a pinch, but it definitely makes the project more time-intensive. You can also adapt the drawings here to accommodate the uncut 1×6 boards.

Start by cutting the side stretchers and legs to length (and width). Place the pieces on your work surface, and place them together spaced as shown in the diagram. Mark the height of the back leg at $23\frac{1}{2}$" and the mark the height of the front leg at $21\frac{1}{2}$". Then connect the points to define the angle at the top of the side leg assembly. We're marking this angle before the sides are assembled, because we need to make sure the pocket screws used to assemble the sides are located to provide the most strength. Be sure you make a left side and a right side. Otherwise you end up with pocket screws showing on the outside!

With the sides marked, I used my Kreg jig to drill pocket holes in the stretchers (two per end on the middle and lower stretchers, and on the top stretchers, two in the back and one in the front. Then I used a clamp to hold the side pieces tight and drove the screws into the legs. Again make sure you've got one left and one right side.

THE RIGHT SLANT

I used a jigsaw to cut the top angle on each side. While this edge will be somewhat hidden by the arms, it's still best to make the cut slow and even for the best edge possible. You may want to touch up the edge with your bench plane.

Even though this was destined to be an outdoor project for me, I still opted to countersink the screw holes and add plugs. I knew it would give the chairs a more "finished" look. I located all the positions of the front and rear stretchers on the sides. Follow the diagrams to mark these locations, then drill the countersink holes for each stretcher in the sides.

3 I used a parallel jaw clamp to hold each side frame tightly together as I inserted the screws.

4 With both sides assembled, I double-checked my top lines for the arm slope.

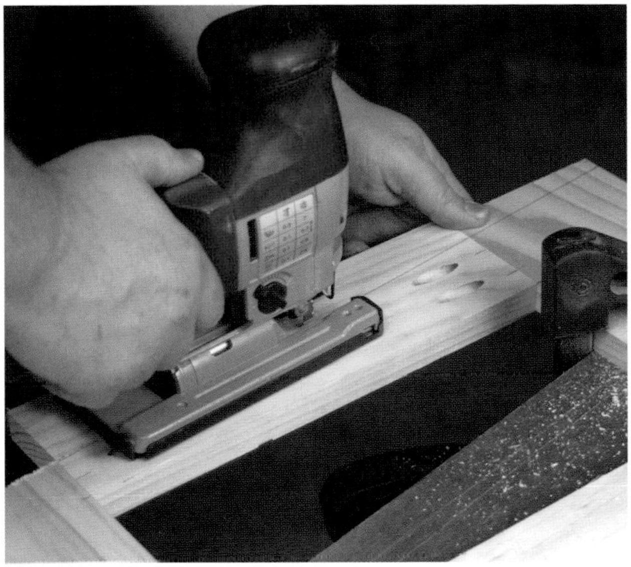

5 I used my jigsaw to cut each slope, staying slightly proud of the line, and then cleaned up the edge with my bench plane.

6 The four stretchers are screwed in place through the sides. I used my countersinking pilot bit to make the clearance holes, anticipating plugging the holes afterward.

7 Holding the two sides together with the stretchers as you drive the screws home can be a bit of a juggle. A clamp or two, and using the other stretchers as spacers makes things more manageable.

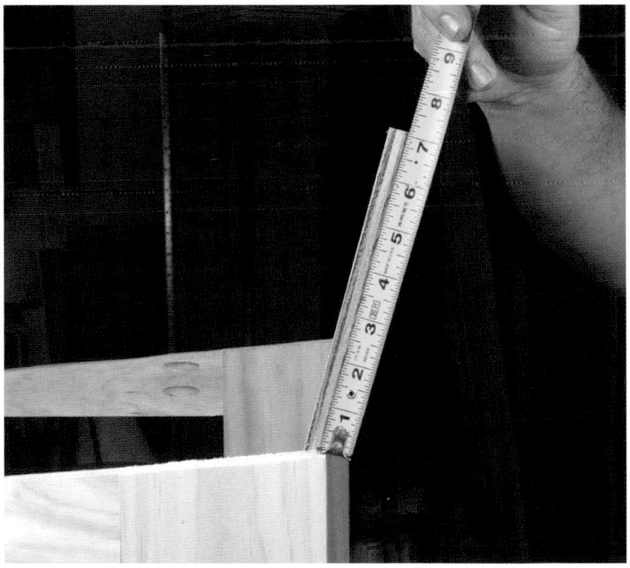

8 I slipped the plywood back in place to test the fit, allowing the back to touch the top point of the side, and extend 7" above the sides.

A clamp or two help hold things in place as you screw the stretchers between the two sides. It helps to use the other stretchers as spacers as you screw.

With your chair looking more cube-like, it's time to cut the plywood back to size using your circular saw. Then position the back between the sides with the height 7" above the seat back, and with the back resting against the back stretcher. Mark the location of the back on the sides, from the inside surfaces. Then remove the back and drill two clearance holes through the sides, stopping before the bit countersinks. Then work from the outside of the side assemblies and drill back through those holes, to countersink from the outside surface.

To finish the back, I marked 1½" radii at the top two corners. I then trimmed the corners to shape with my jigsaw.

LET'S TRY THIS AGAIN

Here's where my planning failed. After screwing the back in place, I was using my daughter to test-sit the chair, and found that a reasonable amount of pressure against the back could force the plywood to split at the screw locations. I could have moved up to a ¾"-thick plywood back, but I liked the look and feel of the thinner ply, so I opted to add ¾" × ¾" bracing cleats behind the back, on both sides. I cut a long taper on each cleat to match the angle at the back. Then I counter-drilled the holes and screwed the cleats in place. More test-sit-

9 The lower part of the back is braced against the back stretcher for more support. I then marked the location of the back on the inside surface of the sides.

10 With the back removed, I drilled two holes through each side, stopping with just the bit poking through the outside surface.

11 I then came from the outside surface of the sides, drilling deeper to countersink the holes for plugs.

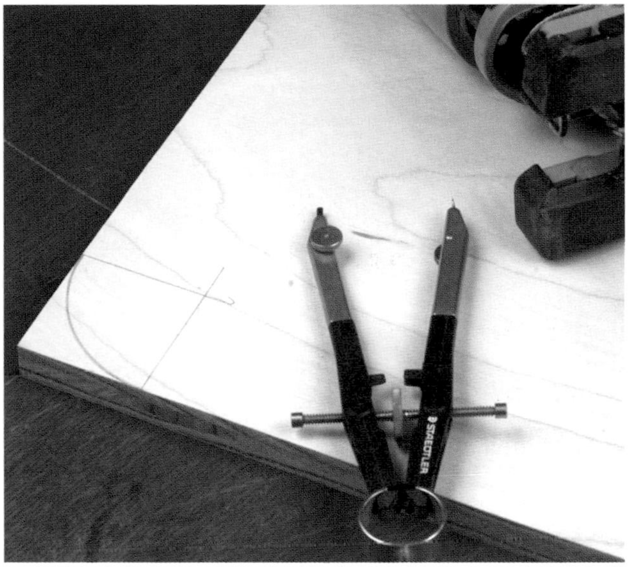

12 With the back removed, I took the opportunity to mark each top corner with a 1¼"-radius and then used my jigsaw to make the cuts, rounding the corners.

13 Next, I screwed the back in place and discovered a problem, The back wasn't thick enough to support the screw without the concern (as shown) of forcing the ply's apart when someone sits in the chair.

14 To add two braces behind the back I used a scrap piece of pine. I cut an angle on the braces so they wouldn't protrude beyond the sides. I used a Japanese dozuki saw to start the cut slowly.

15 After a moment or two, my scrap piece was cut in two.

16 I then marked both pieces for length, and made the cuts.

17 Some glue, a spring clamp and a couple of screws (in countersunk holes) added the braces and made the back much stronger.

18 I then cut the seat slats to length and used my router to round over two long and one short edge on the top of the slats.

19 The slats were then screwed in place through the back stretcher of the chair. I used another scrap piece to hold the side slats ¾" off the side frame, then evenly spaced the other two slats between them. I used an 18-gauge pneumatic pin nailer to attach the front of the slats to the front stretcher. You could also use countersunk screws, or brad nails for this step.

ting proved that the fix was good, and not too ugly.

I moved on to the seat slats next. These too I ended up ripping to 4½"-wide, though you could also use five 1×4s and adjust the spacing between the boards. As this is the place where the hide meets the pine, I added ¼" radius roundovers to the top edges of the seat slats. The slats were then attached using screws through the back stretcher at the back end, and finishing nails through the front edge and down into the front stretcher. Screws at the front of the slats are prone to scratching legs.

ARMING THE CHAIR

For the chair arms, I again added a roundover to the top edges, and then counter-drilled in four spots to attach the arm to the top of each side assembly.

Using the template on page 85, lay out the corbels and cut to shape with a jigsaw. If you have a band saw available, these pieces are an easier cut with the larger machine. I counter-drilled one hole from the inside to mount the corbels (a little glue here is a good idea), then added another screw to the corbel through the top of each arm.

FINISHING TOUCHES

There are 50 holes in the chair, and I wanted them to disappear once the paint was on, so that meant 50, ⅜" wood plugs are glued in place, and then sanded flush (which took a little bit of time).

After the plugs are sanded flush, the whole chair needs a good sanding. Wherever two flat surfaces mate (such as the area shown in photo 20 at the right) this should be sanded as flush as possible. Assuming that you're using a solid color paint as I did, each of these mating edges will show up more dramatically than you might expect.

You should also spend a little time to take break all the edges of the chair to make it more comfortable to the touch. This is one of those steps that makes a huge difference. Sharp edges aren't worth rushing to the end of the project.

The last step is the paint. As you may have noticed in the opening photo, I built two of these chairs, and the first one was painted with a can of spray paint in a brown color. The spray paint didn't cover the surfaces as well as I prefered, and to be honest I wasn't too crazy about the color. So back to the store and I chose a quart of the red shown. It was worth the extra work.

20 I next used my router to round over the top edges of the arms. I then pre-drilled and countersunk holes in the arms, and screwed them in place to the top of the sides. (Yes, that's Pete Townsend watching over my work.)

21 Use the template to mark and cut out the arm support corbels. A jigsaw works, but if you've got a band saw handy, it's easier. Sand the corbels, and then add some glue and screw them in place through the inside surface of the side frames. I held my corbels about ¼" back from the front edge.

22 Now screw down through the arm and into the top of the corbel.

23 One of the longer steps is plugging all the screw holes and then sanding them flush. It's worth it to give the piece a finished look.

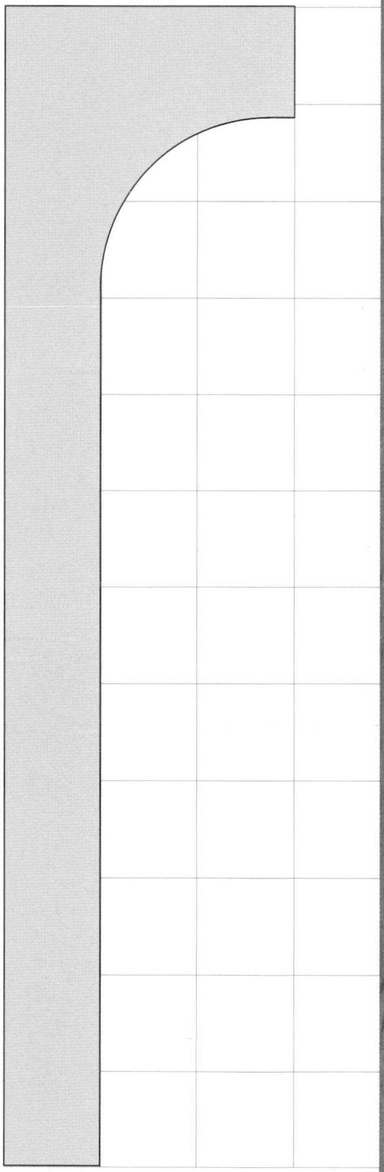

Each square = ½"

ALL-WEATHER MORRIS CHAIR

10

If you read the introduction to this book, then you know that this next project is special to me. It was the spark for all of my one-by furniture designs, and is still the most comfortable. The original All Weather Morris Chair was designed to fit a seat and back cushion. This made the chair comfortable, but if it had just rained and the cushions were wet, the bare chair wasn't designed for sitting comfortably. The chair shown here is version 4.0 and I've modified it to work with, or without cushions, and I've adjusted some design and building techniques. I think it's an excellent upgrade. Oh, did I mention the price? Built from pine, each chair runs about $60 in materials, plus the cost of the hinge. A good coat of exterior paint and you've got a great chair for under $100.

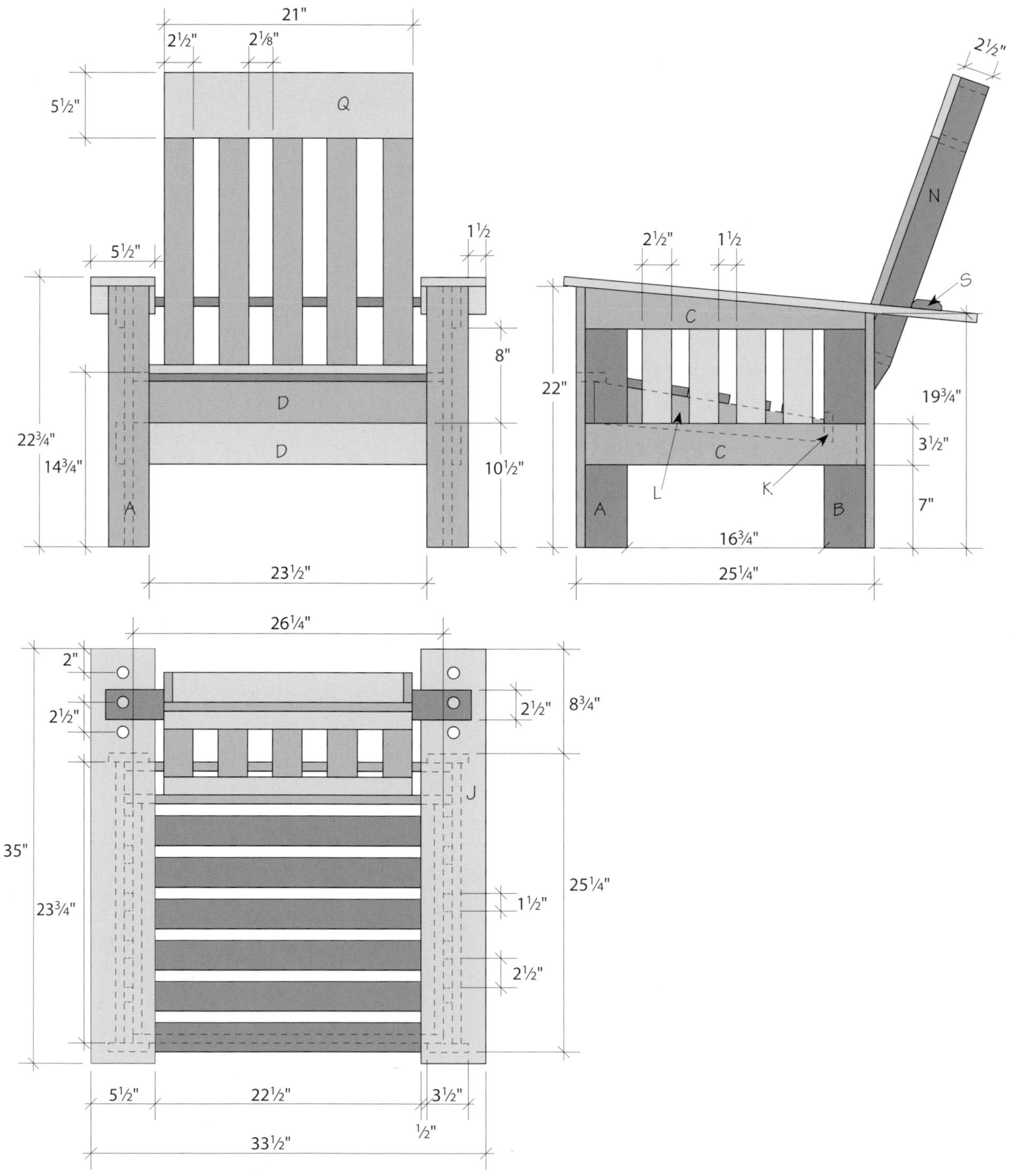

21"
2½"
2⅛"
5½"
Q
5½"
1½
22¾"
14¾"
8"
D
D
10½"
A
23½"
2½"
2½"
1½
N
S
C
22"
19¾"
3½"
C
L
K
7"
A
B
16¾"
25¼"
26¼"
2"
2½"
2½"
8¾"
J
35"
23¾"
25¼"
1½"
2½"
5½"
22½"
3½"
½"
33½"

ALL-WEATHER MORRIS CHAIR • INCHES (MILLIMETERS)

REFERENCE	QUANTITY	PART	STOCK	THICKNESS	(mm)	WIDTH	(mm)	LENGTH	(mm)
A	4	front legs*	pine	3/4	19	3 1/2	89	22	559
B	4	rear legs*	pine	3/4	19	3 1/2	89	20	508
C	4	side strtchrs**	pine	3/4	19	3 1/2	89	23 3/4	603
D	2	f&b stretchers	pine	3/4	19	3 1/2	89	26 1/4	667
E	2	side slats*	pine	3/4	19	2 1/2	64	14 1/2	368
F	2	side slats*	pine	3/4	19	2 1/2	64	14 1/8	359
G	2	side slats*	pine	3/4	19	2 1/2	64	13 3/4	349
H	2	side slats*	pine	3/4	19	2 1/2	64	13 1/2	343
J	2	arms	pine	3/4	19	5 1/2	140	35	889
K	1	rear support	pine	3/4	19	2 1/2	64	26 1/4	667
L	2	side spprts***	pine	3/4	19	5 1/2	140	19 1/2	495
M	6	seat slats	pine	3/4	19	2 1/2	64	26 1/4	667
N	2	back frame	pine	3/4	19	2 1/2	64	30	762
P	3	back frame	pine	3/4	19	2 1/2	64	19 1/2	495
Q	2	back plates	pine	3/4	19	5 1/2	140	21	533
R	5	back slats	pine	3/4	19	2 1/2	64	19	483
S	1	back suppport	pine	3/4	19	2 1/2	64	31	787
T	2	dowels	hrdwd	1D	25			2	51

* 5° angle, one end

** 5° slope on top edge of two

*** Cut to match template.

You might notice that the lumber in the photos looks a little weird. It is. Half of it is over 40 years old. In rehabbing our house, I pulled out some old pine closets. Rather than throw the boards away, I tucked them aside, and when this project came around, I knew I could be earth conscious and reuse them. Since the whole piece was getting painted, no one would be the wiser. I did cut all the pieces to standard home center sizes, so I wasn't cheating.

There are a lot of pieces to this chair, but if you go ahead and cut them all to length, assembly will move pretty quickly.

BUILDING THE LEGS

Each of the legs is made of two pieces of wood screwed together length-wise to create a T-shape.

1 The T-shaped front and back legs have a 5° bevel at the top. It's easiest to cut that bevel before assembly. With the four front- and rear-facing pieces cut to the length given in the cutting list, set the saw for a 5° bevel and trim one end of each piece.

But to give the chairs their backward slope, the tops of the legs are cut back at a 5° angle. This means the front legs (with the flat piece facing forward) need a 5° angle on the top edge of the front piece, across the thickness of the board. The leg of the T that fits behind the front piece, needs a 5° cut from the front-to-back on the width of the board. This process is reversed on the two back legs, since the flat piece is to the rear of the leg. Take your time marking and identifying the angles before making the cuts with your miter saw.

The chair is essentially screwed together. I used a countersink bit to drill clearance holes and recesses for wood plugs in one motion.

Start by marking the center of each flat piece of the front and back legs. Drill the countersink holes and screw the legs together.

MAKING THE SIDES

To join the front and back legs to create left and right leg sets, mark up 7" on the outside of each leg. Make sure you have front and back pairs. Then screw the two lower side stretchers in place on the legs.

The upper side stretchers will require a 5° slope on the top edge. Place an upper stretcher in position, flush with the top edge of the front leg, and make sure the space between the stretchers is even at front and back. Then make a mark at the leg heights at both the front and back ends of the upper stretcher.

2 Transfer the bevel location from the four cut pieces to the side-facing pieces of the legs. Remember that the front and rear legs are mirror images of one another, with the shorter "leg" pair to the rear. The legs are shown above positioned as they will be, with the rear (shorter) set on the left. The L's will become T's when the horizontal pieces are screwed to the center of the vertical pieces.

3 After marking the bevel locations, cut the other four pieces on the flat.

4 All four legs have the leg of the T centered on the flat of the T. Mark the center line for screws.

5 Drill three or four countersunk holes in each leg flat.

6 Then screw the leg pairs together, flushing the bevel ends to form the T. Pilot drill and countersink to avoid splitting.

7 The lower side stretchers are located up 7″ from the bottom of each leg.

Connect the two marks to create a straight line, then cut the angle with a jigsaw. Clean up the cut with a bench plane if necessary. Mark the other upper stretcher the same way, then cut the slope.

Screw each upper stretcher in place on the outside of each leg, and you're getting closer.

To create the box of the chair, the front and back stretchers are screwed in place with the front stretcher located 10½" up on the inside of the front legs. The back stretcher is located 7" up on the inside of the back legs.

SIDE SLATS

The next step is to attach the side slats. You'll see that I've provided individual lengths for each slat in the cutting list. Each slat also gets a 5° angle cut on the top edge. I've found it easiest to mark the locations of the slats (spaced 1⅜" apart, starting from the back of the front leg), then hold the slat in place and mark the angle on the top of each slat.

Because I want each slat top flush to the top of the upper side stretcher, I cut the slats a little short, letting the bottom of the slat fit up slightly from the bottom edge of the lower side stretchers.

Screw the slats in place with a single screw at top and bottom. I couldn't countersink these screws because the two ¾"-thick pieces don't allow enough room to add a plug. If you want to hide the screws, then you will need to add wood putty and then sand it

8 Screw the side stretchers in place on the outside of the legs.

9 Space the upper side stretcher 8" above the lower stretcher, which should be even at the top edge with the top edge of the front leg.

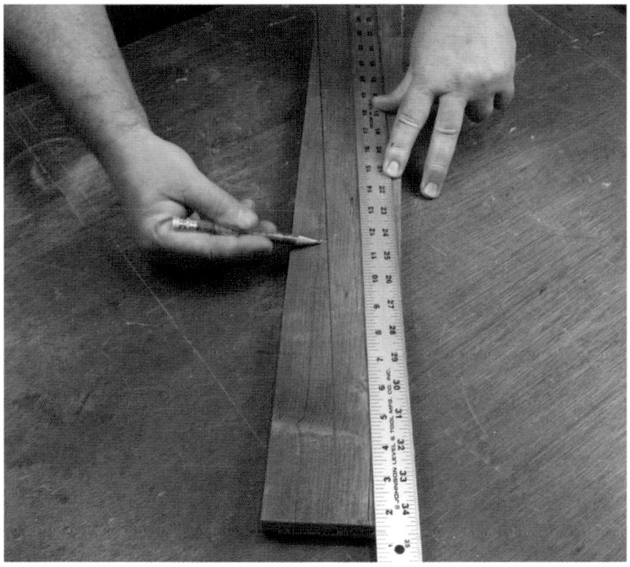

10 Connect your front and rear marks with a straight edge.

11 Jigsaw wide of your pencil mark to leave room for cleanup.

12 Screw the upper stretchers in place to complete the leg sides.

13 The front and back stretchers are screwed in place to the front and back legs. Check for squareness where the stretchers meet the legs.

14 I prefer to mark the slat lengths with each slat held in place.

15 A single screw in the center of each slat (top and bottom) holds things comfortably in place.

16 The seat supports fit flush to the top of the front stretcher, and attach to the slats.

17 At the rear of the seat support, a 1 x 3 is screwed in place between the two legs. Another screw from the rear holds the piece against the ends of the supports.

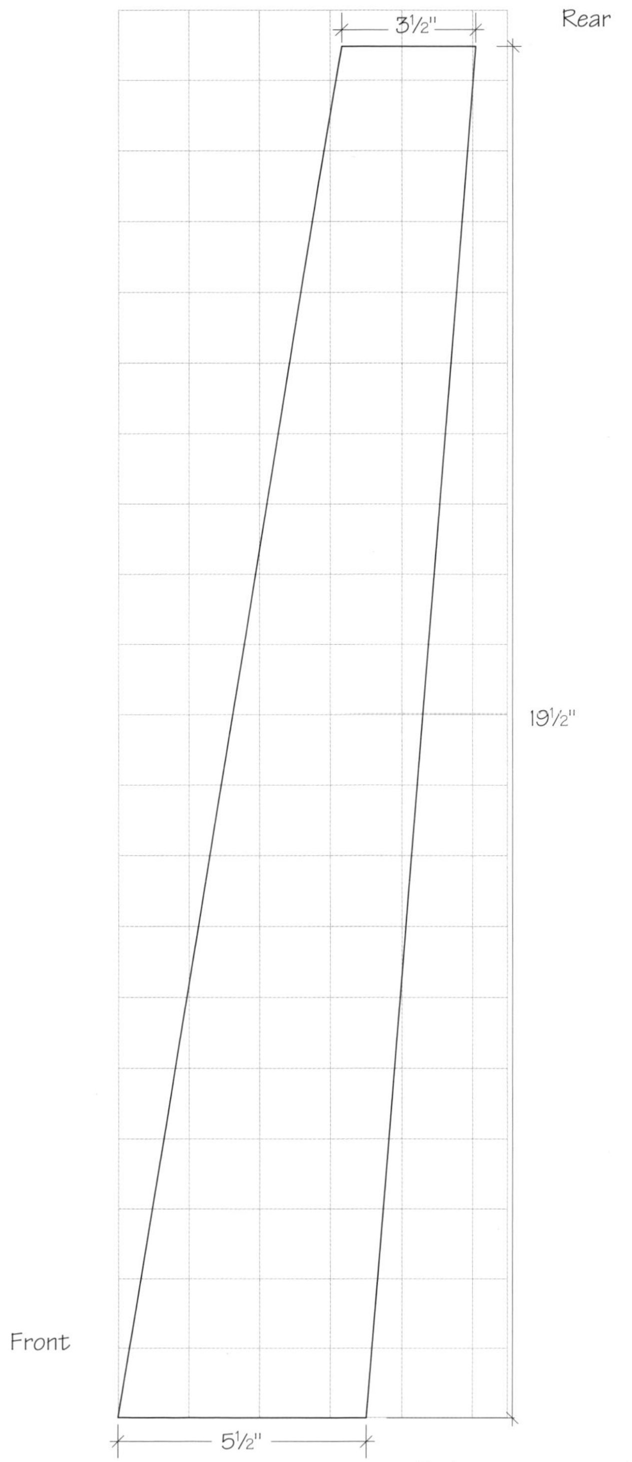

Side Support Template

Each square represents 1".

smooth. I just allowed the paint to hide the screw heads.

SIDE SUPPORTS

With the slats in place, I checked the pattern (shown at left) for the shape of each side seat support. Though the supports are cut from 1×6 boards, the only cuts necessary are on the two long edges. The short ends keep the "squared" cuts from cutting the 1×6's to length. Transfer the pattern to your board and cut the side supports to shape with your jigsaw.

Clean up the cut edges with a hand plane, then screw the supports in place on each side.

One last piece to hold things together. The rear support is the piece that will support the back frame of the chair. It's essentially a mount for the hinge. It's screwed between the two rear legs, and tight up against the back end of the two seat side supports. This piece is screwed through the back legs, and through the back support into the ends of the side supports.

MORE SLATS AND ARMS

We're now ready to add the seat slats. This is pretty straightforward, with the slats spaced 1" apart. The front slat is notched ⅞"-deep to fit around the front legs, and then is screwed in place to the front stretcher. This allows an overhang on the front slat. The front slat gets four screws, but all the others get two. A single screw on each end. I countersunk these holes for plugs.

The arms seem to bring things more than a step further somehow. One of the things that makes a Morris chair special is the ability to recline the back. To make this simple, three holes are drilled in the arms to offer three reclining positions. The holes are centered and at the back of each arm. The back support has two dowels attached that fit into the holes. This is also the reason why the arms extend so far beyond the back of the seat, and it's one of the things that makes this chair a Morris! Clever folks! The arms should overhang the legs 1" at the front and by 1½" on the outside edges.

BUILDING THE BACK

The chair back is screwed together (countersink for plugs) with three horizontal cross members. The two at the top are spaced to fit a headrest plate, and the bottom to accommodate a matching plate (for symmetry). Both the plates should cover only half of the horizontal cross member, allowing you to nail or screw both the plates and the back slats to the same cross member.

With the cross members positioned correctly, screw them in place through the back's frame sides. Next screw the top and bottom plates in place.

Lastly, to allow the proper swing of the back, clip the back corners of the seat at a 45° angle with your jigsaw.

To complete the back, simply screw the slats in place on the frame. The two outside slats are

18 After notching the front seat slat to fit around the legs, I used a roundover bit in my trim router to round the long edges of each slat. Less chance of pinching something important.

19 The front slat is screwed in place on the front stretcher.

20 The rest of the seat slats are screwed into the seat supports on either side

21 The two arms are also rounded with the router, Then screwed in place.

22 Three cross members are screwed in place between the two frame sides.

23 The top and bottom plates are then screwed to the front of the frame, lipping only half way over the two middle cross members.

held flush to the sides of the back, with the other slats spaced evenly between. You'll notice a difference between the illustrations and the picture. On the chair in the front photo I used three 3½"-width slats, with two 2½" slats between. Either design is fine, I just decided to play a bit with the spacing. Feel free to be creative with your chair!

I rounded over the top edges of the back support (using my trim router), then drilled two ¼"-deep holes marked directly from the holes on the chair arms. By doing this rather than measuring, I'm assured a proper fit.

Next, the two 2"-long pieces of 1"-diameter dowels are screwed in place on the back support.

A good final sanding to all surfaces and I was ready to paint. Any decent Krylon color will put a great finish on the chair. I used spray cans, and honestly, it took about six, so prepare for that.

The last step is to mount the back to the chair. I've used a variety of hinges over the years, but I've found I get the best look and performance from a continuous, or piano, hinge.

That's it! You're ready to kick back and enjoy the day.

24 A 45-degree cut at the bottom of the back allows the back to swing to full-back position.

25 The back slats are then screwed in place.

26 After carefully marking the location for the dowels on the back support, I drill a shallow hole to protect the top of the dowel from the weather, and to locate the dowel accurately.

27 The 2" chunk of dowel can then be glued (if you prefer) and/or screwed in place.

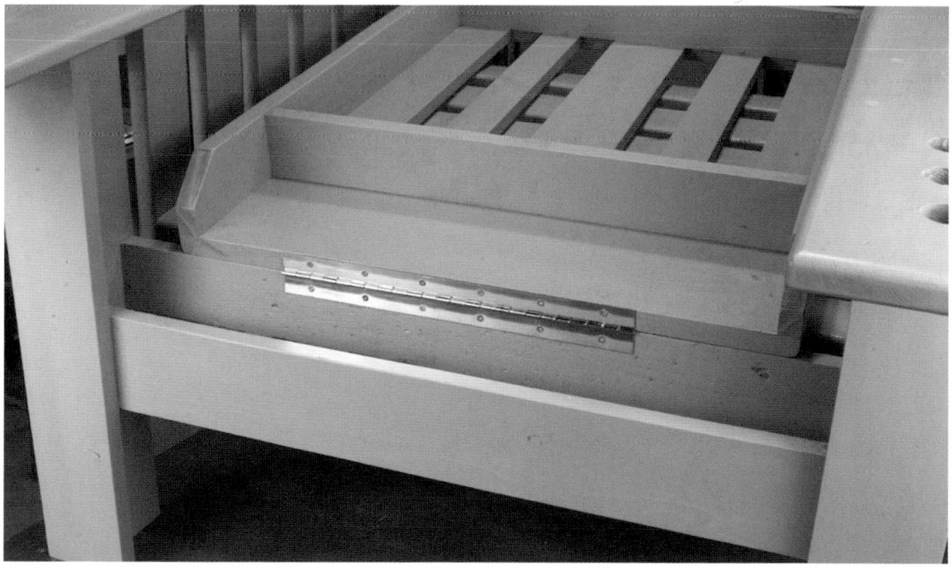

28 After painting, the last step is to screw the continuous hinge to the back, then rest it in place on the chair and screw the other leaf of the hinge in place on the back seat suppot.

STICKLEY SPLAYED TABORET

11

I ran across the original of this early Gustav Stickley piece on the internet (referred to as a Tom Jones Drink Stand) a while back and thought is was a stunning design. The sculpted and tapered legs combine to give the small table an organic and deceiving look. Originally built of white oak, I opted for poplar with an ebonized finish. The finished size is close to the original (and the re-issue from The Stickley Company), though I added 4" to the width of the top to make it more of a plant stand than a drink stand. The original included carvings at the top of the legs, and I've adjusted the shape of the legs. I also can't swear to the accuracy of the 5° taper, but the finished look is good.

Beyond the design, the simplicity of the construction also caught my eye. While Gus no doubt would have used wedged tenons, or a hidden tenon, screws and plugs worked pretty well for my version.

The hardest part of this project was designing the shape of the legs. Luckily, you have the benefit of a scaled drawing (on page 105) of the leg shape, so I've saved you some effort.

Start by gluing-up the pieces for the top and shelf. The sizes forced me to glue up slightly bigger panels (using the standard home center sizes) than I preferred, so there was some waste when they were cut to finished size. I still think the finished look makes it worth the effort, and honestly the materials for the table ran about $45. A single 1×8×10' will do the whole table.

Next move to the legs. Start by transferring the leg pattern to a full-size template. ¼" plywood or hardboard are great, but cardboard will do in a pinch. Cut the template to shape, then transfer the shape to the legs.

While the legs are still rectangular, head over to your miter saw and cut 5° angles on the top and bottom of each leg. This will provide a tight fit to the top, and also let the table rest more evenly on the floor.

With the angles cut, grab your jigsaw and cut the four legs to shape. If you happen to have a shop with a band saw, this step is easier done on that tool. But if you're not so equipped, the jigsaw still does alright.

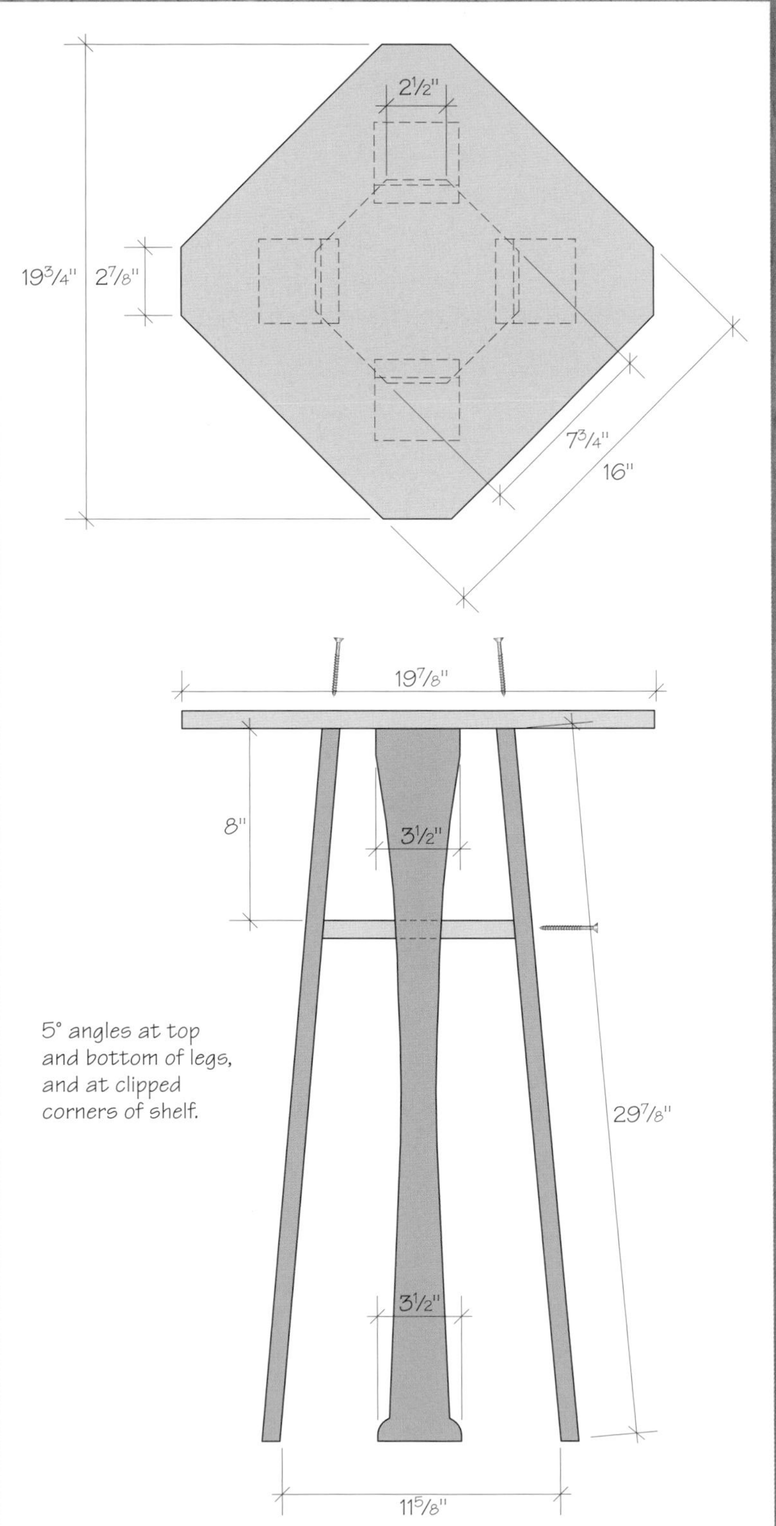

STICKLEY SPLAYED TABORET • INCHES (MILLIMETERS)

REFERENCE	QUANTITY	PART	STOCK	THICKNESS	(mm)	WIDTH	(mm)	LENGTH	(mm)
A	1	top	poplar	3/4	19	18	457	18	457
B	4	legs	poplar	3/4	19	3 1/2	89	28 1/4	718
C	1	shelf	poplar	3/4	19	7 3/4	197	7 3/4	197

1 I started by gluing up three 1×8s for the top blank and two 1×6s for the shelf.

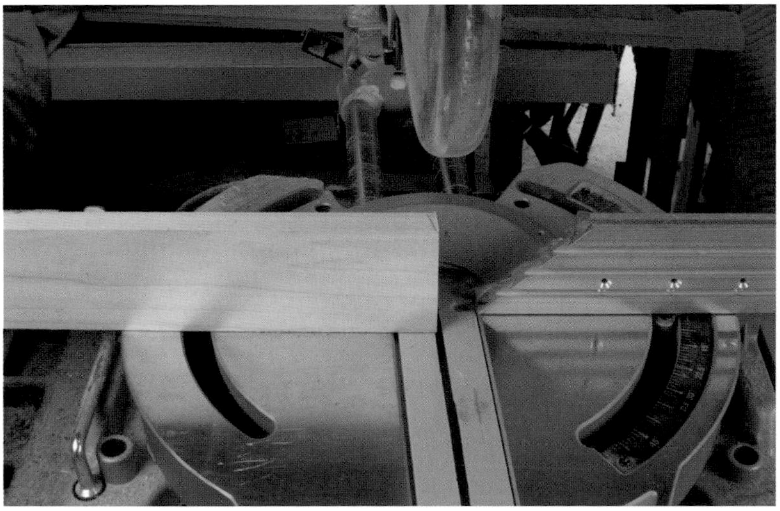

2 Part of creating the splay of the legs are 5° miter cuts on the tops and bottoms of each leg. The top and bottom miter cuts should be parallel to one another after the cuts are made.

While the shapes on the legs don't need to be exact duplicates, it does give a better finished look. If Gus were building them today, he'd be looking to his CNC (Computer Numerical Control) machine to knock these out quickly. Even without that technology, a large run of these tables would benefit from a pattern-routing set up. But for one, I simply clamped the four legs together and went to work with a random orbit sander and a set of wood files to get all four legs close in shape. While you're sanding, it's a good idea to finish sand the insides and edges of the legs, and also the shelf and underside of the top. It's impossible to do this step once the table is assembled.

After cleaning up the legs, I carefully marked the location of the shelf on each leg. A single screw (countersunk) will hold each leg in place against the shelf.

The shelf itself needs to have the four corners cut at a 45° angle across the top face, and at a 5° angle from top to bottom (leaving a 2" width). This gives the legs the tapered look. I used my miter saw and a simple jig to help with this step. Next, screw the legs in place one leg at a time.

The top was a little big to fit on the miter saw, so I cut the 45° corners with my jigsaw.

I chose to attach the top to the legs by simply screwing down through the top, using wood plugs to hide the screws. You could also use glue and dowels if you didn't want plugs showing on your top.

To locate the screw holes, I flipped the top upside down, then positioned the base on the top, marking the leg locations.

Since my marks were on the underside of the top, I used a small drill bit to drill up through the top at a slight angle, creating two holes for each leg. I then flipped over the top and used my countersinking bit (guided by the smaller holes) to create the screw holes in the top.

Eight screws through the top and you've got a table! I plugged all the screw holes, then gave the table a final sanding.

The finish for this piece is Minwax Ebony Wood Stain (not gel). If you have poplar boards with uneven coloring (green and white mixed), you may be able to see the green showing slightly through the ebony finish. A top coat of semi-gloss spray lacquer finishes it off. I do like this table!

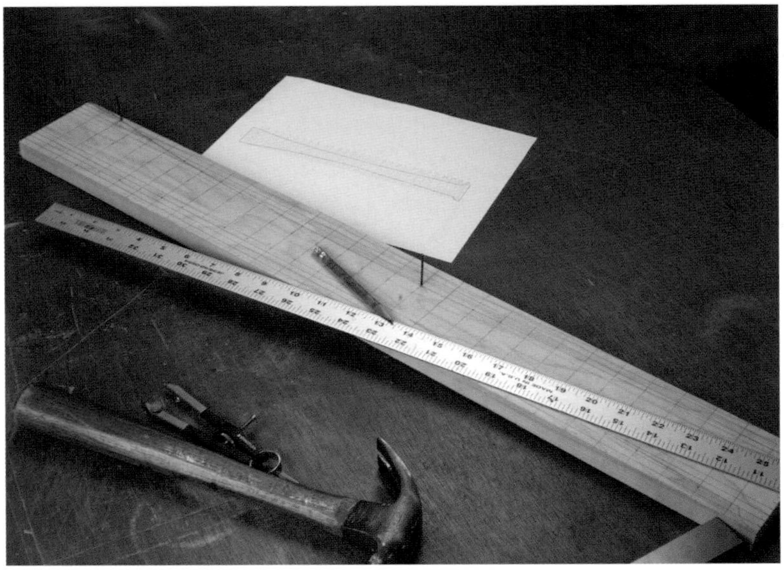

3 Using a steel rule and compass, I transferred the leg shape to a template. Actually I used one of the legs, but I recommend you use a template.

4 Trim the legs to shape with your jigsaw, cutting slightly wide of the line to allow for clean-up.

5 To get the legs close to uniform in shape, I clamped them together and used a random orbit sander to clean up the legs all at once.

6 I used a 45° guide on my miter saw to help clip the corners on the shelf piece.

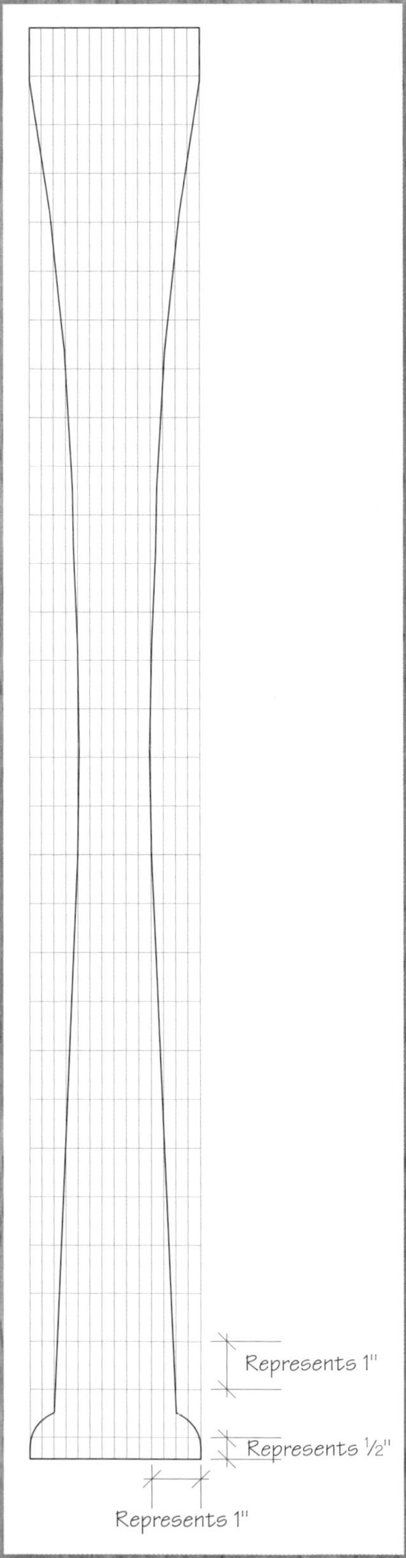

7 A single countersunk hole in each leg allows the legs to be screwed to the shelf.

8 Start with a single leg...

9 ...then add a leg at a time, working on a flat surface to keep the legs sitting evenly.

10 I used my jigsaw to make the 45° cuts on the corners of the top (no 5° slope required).

11 I then located the leg positions on the underside of the top, by setting the base in place and measuring to allow even spacing on all sides.

12 Pilot holes, drilled from the bottom of the top, set the screw locations.

13 A countersunk bit from above gets you ready to finish the table.

PHILISTINE

ENTRY HALL BENCH

12

One of the benchmarks (sorry, couldn't resist) of Arts & Crafts furniture is the settle. Or as we'd call it, the couch. They were built in a broad variety of styles. Box, armless, spindle-back, through-posts, prairie, heavy and petite. But one piece that I was interested in building was more of a hall entry bench with storage in the seat. This, it seems, was much less common.

After spending a significant amount of time searching books and the internet, I stumbled across an image of this bench. Not exactly this bench, but one with the general details. I'm embarrassed to say that I've lost the original image, and the website (computers and teens), but the CAD illustration I drew (with my adaptations) was rescued.

The size is just right. The storage is adequate for a few things, but not so big that you won't be able to find what's at the bottom. It will take a simple cushion (if that's your desire), or can stay bare for a mud-room setting. And, of course, it's made only with materials from the home center store; 1× oak boards, a small section of oak plywood and a small section of pegboard for the inside bottom.

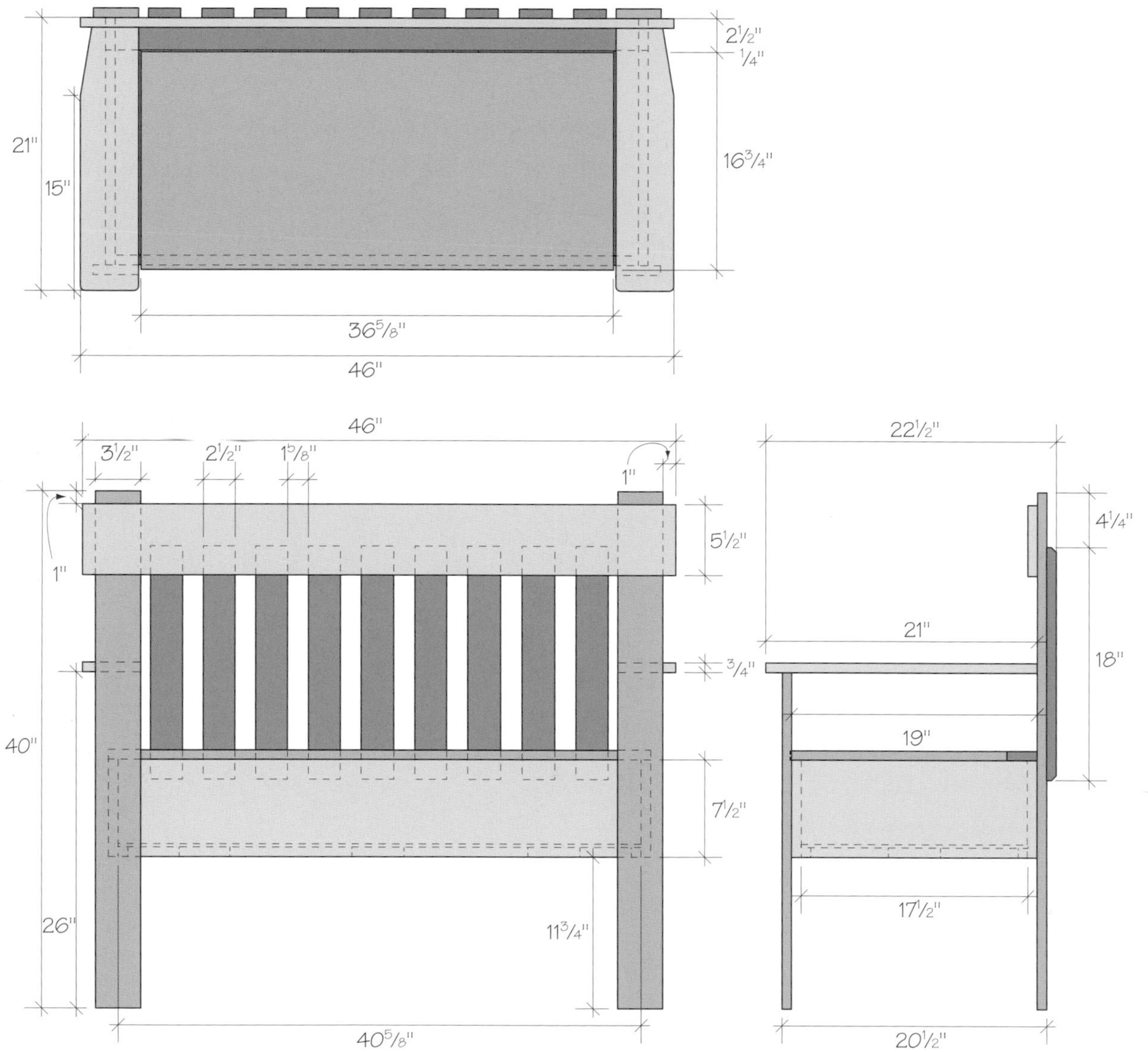
21"
15"
2½"
¼"
16¾"
36⅝"
46"
46"
3½"
2½"
1⅝"
1"
1"
5½"
¾"
40"
7½"
26"
11¾"
40⅝"
22½"
4¼"
21"
18"
19"
17½"
20½"

ENTRY HALL BENCH • INCHES (MILLIMETERS)

REFERENCE	QUANTITY	PART	STOCK	THICKNESS	(mm)	WIDTH	(mm)	LENGTH	(mm)
A	2	front legs	oak	3/4	19	3 1/2	89	26	660
B	2	rear legs	oak	3/4	19	3 1/2	89	40	1016
C	1	back rest	oak	3/4	19	5 1/2	140	46	1168
D	2	box sides	oak	3/4	19	7 1/2	191	19	483
E	2	box front/back	oak	3/4	19	7 1/2	191	40 5/8	1032
F	2	arms	oak	3/4	19	4 1/2	114	21	533
G	9	back slats	oak	3/4	19	2 1/2	64	18*	457
H	1	seat back rail	oak	3/4	19	2 1/2	64	42 3/4	1086
I	2	seat side rails	oak	3/4	19	2 1/2	64	16 1/2**	419
J	1	seat	plywd	3/4	19	16 3/4	425	36 5/8	984
K	1	box bottom	pegbd	1/4	6	17 1/2	445	40 1/2	1029
L	8	bottom cleats	oak	3/4	19	3/4	19	4	102

* Face chamfers both ends

** Cut to fit

BUILDING THE BOX

The construction of the bench starts with a box made from 1×6 oak and pocket screwed together. The front legs are then screwed to the box, then the rear legs. The seat frame is screwed together with pocket screws and glued in place on the seat box. A back rest is added, then arms and back slats. Lastly the plywood seat is hinged in place.

Construction starts with my Kreg pocket jig. I leave the jig set up with the bit and screw-driving blade sitting in the holes. It takes just a minute to be drilling holes. Luckily I had clamps long enough to hold the box pieces in place as I put the screws in. If you're not so lucky, clamp the

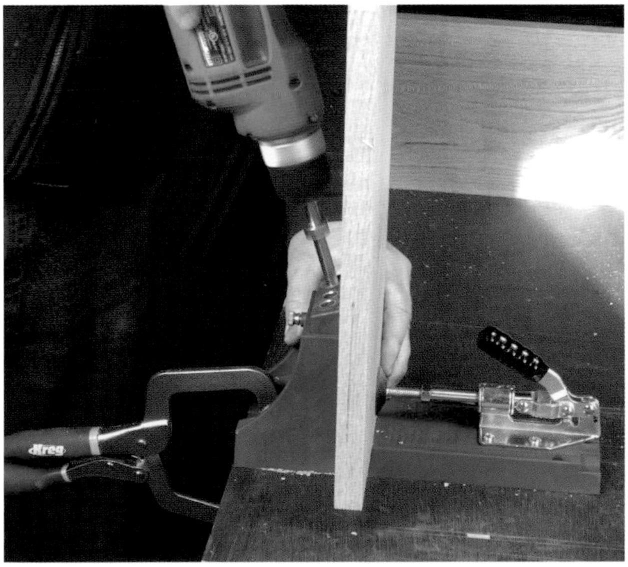

1 Functional boxes, such as the gloves and scarf storage built into this bench, don't usually have to be pretty on the inside. That's why pocket screws are a solid construction technique for this storage.

2 Use a clamp (if you have one long enough) to hold the front and back panels between the end pieces. The legs will hide the joint, leaving a full panel visible from the ends of the bench.

3 Clamp one of the front legs in place, allowing about a 1" overhang on each end of the seat box. Mark the location of the legs so you won't have to measure when you screw the leg in place.

4 Staggered drywall screws attach the front legs to the box. Because I was screwing two 1x pieces together, flat to one another, I couldn't easily use a piloted countersink to drill the holes. So I pre-drilled through the inside of the box, used a countersink bit to recess the surface, then screwed the legs on. The "finished" shot here shows the screws after I've taken the clamps off. Repeat for the other front leg.

5 The same process is used for the back legs. Allow the bench to rest on the front legs while attaching the first back leg. This will give you the chance to check the level of the bench before screwing the leg in place. Then clamp the fourth leg in place with the bench on a flat surface and adjust the leg to keep the bench sitting stable. Then screw the fourth leg in place.

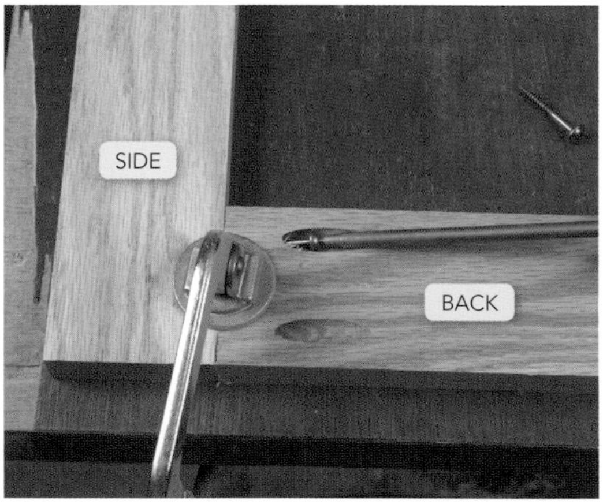

6 The three-piece, U-shaped frame surrounding the seat is held together at the corners with pocket screws. The shorter side pieces run through from the back of the front leg, to the front of the back leg. The back piece runs between the two side pieces.

7 To avoid difficulty getting the frame to fit flush to the ends, allow the frame to extend an 1/8" over, creating a small overhang. Then glue the frame in place.

8 Next, screw the back rest in place to the back legs, holding the legs 1" in from the ends and the back 1" down from the top of the legs. Again because of the flat-to-flat orientation of the boards, I didn't trust my piloted countersink bit to not come through the front, so I pre-drilled the holes, countersunk them and put the screws in. If your bench back will be visible, some wood putty, or oak buttons can be used to hide the screws.

end to your workbench so you can lean into the long pieces as you place the screw. A little bit of tape on the outside corner of the joint can hold things in place for a minute, if you're having trouble.

GIVING IT LEGS

With the box assembled, the front, then rear legs are attached. In my attempt to keep the designs as "light" as possible, I've used a few flat-to-flat board face joints, such as with attaching the legs. As I'm using 1¼"-long drywall screws, I'm left with only ¼" of comfort space before I screw through the opposite (and most visible) face. This makes using a countersinking bit and filling the hole with a wood plug very difficult. For these flat-to-flat joints, I'll let you decide whether wood putty, or a wood button (or nothing at all) is your preference to hide the screws.

As you attach the legs, work on a flat surface when attaching the back legs to keep the bench sitting level.

To allow the seat to hinge and lift open, it needs to clear the edges of the arms. To make this work, I added a frame to complete the horizontal surface of the seat deck. Having the frame run at the back of the bench also allows the seat to tilt back slightly and stand open when in use. The frame is held together with pocket screws, then glued to the seat box.

Next, the back rest is simply screwed to the back legs.

After adding a "slimming" angle to the back edge of the arms, they are also screwed in place, followed quickly by the back slats. Now it's starting to look like a bench.

MAKING THE STORAGE

We still need to add a bottom for the seat section. I chose to use hardboard pegboard for a couple of reasons. It's inexpensive, durable when used in a small enough size, or when mounted securely, and it allows air movement in the storage area. There may very well be cold, wet things tossed in the bench, and we don't want them to mildew. Then you're ready to fit the seat, add veneer tape, and screw the seat in place.

AND FINALLY, A FINISH

A thorough sanding of the entire piece to 120 grit, and I was ready to add color. I used Minwax Jacobean stain to give the bench a fairly dark look, then wiped on a couple of coats of Minwax clear satin wipe-on polyurethane finish, sanding with No. 0000 steel wool between coats.

9 To make the arms more graceful, I mark the back corner of one arm, 6" up the side, and, while holding the arm in place, make a second mark on the back of the arm, flush with the edge of the back leg. Then connect the dots.

10 Finally I get to use my piloting countersink bit! Two holes in the arms located to intersect with the top of the front legs.

11 Drive the screws home. We'll come back and put the wood plugs in place in a minute.

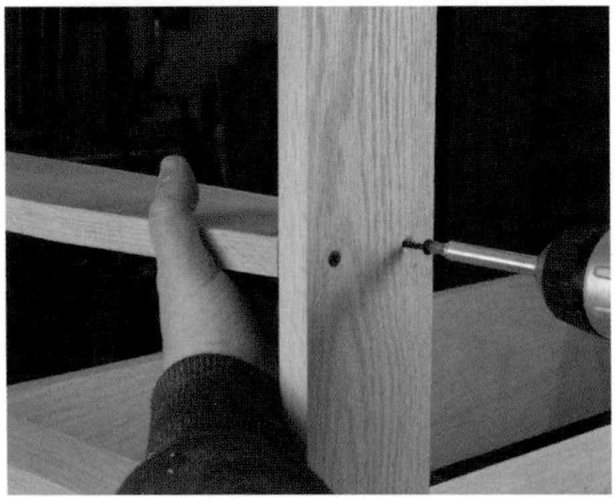

12 Two more countersunk holes in the back leg let us drive two screws into the back of the arm. Now put wood plugs in the four countersunk arm holes, using a dab of glue and light taps with a hammer. We'll sand the plugs flush later.

13 To soften the look of the back slats, each is cut to length and then beveled on a 45° angle at each end to, leaving a ¼" flat.

14 Once again, not deep enough for plugs, each slat is screwed in place in a slightly countersunk hole.

15 Nearing the end. The bottom is cut from the pegboard sheet to fit exactly inside the storage box. A jigsaw or circular saw makes this cut easily manageable. Then scrap strips are cut to length and screwed to the insides of the storage box, flush to the bottom. But before you do that, push the pegboard in place against the underside of the seat frame. It's tough to get the bottom in after the strips are in place. The bottom simply rests on the strips.

16 Fit the plywood seat to the frame opening, holding the front edge of the seat slight back from the front edge of the legs. Allow space for the two leaves of the hinge that will be between the seat and the frame. I added strips of iron-on veneer to the four edges of the seat, sanding them flush to the surfaces. I then used three 12" lengths of brass continuous hinge to attach the seat to the back of the seat frame.

HALL TREE

13

This project was born of necessity as well as desire. When I moved my family of seven into our new house, it came equipped with one coat closet that was about the size of a phone booth (remember them?). The closet was filled immediately, and whenever coats were worn, they ended up thrown on a chair (if I was lucky) in the hall. We needed a coat rack!

Being a fan of Arts & Crafts, I started looking around for an appropriate, historical design. And looked, and looked. Seems that coat racks weren't high on the "design" list. Oh they exist alright, but they're pretty bland. And most were of a single-post design that really didn't give me as much room as I wanted.

One design did come up a few times — referred to as a costumer. This was actually a piece of furniture designed for the bedroom, rather than the hall, and was used to keep clothes tidy between wearings (washing machine?, not in the early 1900s).

I was getting close, but they still weren't attractive. That's when I took all the concepts, looked at a couple of Frank Lloyd Wright designs, and made my own hall tree!

GETTING STARTED

Construction on the hall tree is easy, using biscuits to align the pieces, rather than to provide strength. The biscuit joints are long-grain-to-long-grain joints, so the strength comes from the wood fibers.

The hall tree is made up of six parts and some banding to dress things up. There are the two posts, the two cross beams and the two feet. Construction starts with the two posts, but to hide as much of the joinery (and to gain the most strength) we're going to screw the four pieces that make up the cross beams between the two inside sides of the posts before creating the posts.

HALL TREE • INCHES (MILLIMETERS)

REFERENCE	QUANTITY	PART	STOCK	THICKNESS	(mm)	WIDTH	(mm)	LENGTH	(mm)
A	4	post sides	oak	$^3/_4$	19	$3^1/_2$	89	72	1829
B	4	post sides	oak	$^3/_4$	19	$2^1/_2$	64	72	1829
C	4	cross beams	oak	$^3/_4$	19	$3^1/_2$	89	12	305
D	4	base sides	oak	$^3/_4$	19	$4^1/_2$	115	20	508
E	4	base tops	oak	$^3/_4$	19	$3^1/_2$	89	9*	229
F	4	end caps	oak	$^3/_4$	19	$3^1/_2$	89	$2^1/_8$*	54
G	2	caps	oak	$^3/_4$	19	5	127	$5^1/_2$	14
H		banding	oak	$^3/_4$	19	$^3/_4$	19	aprox. 12′	

* Cut ends to match angle.

1 The first step is cutting most of the pieces to length. The crossbeams (shown above), as well as the eight post pieces, need to be very close to the same length. As close as possible, or it will throw off the squareness of the finished project and make the process more complicated. To acheive this, I cut as many like-length pieces at the same time on my miter saw.

2 The posts are glued together, but biscuits make it possible to align the pieces without things slipping around. I clamped the pieces together to mark the biscuit locations every 12" or so on the edges of the wider post pieces ...

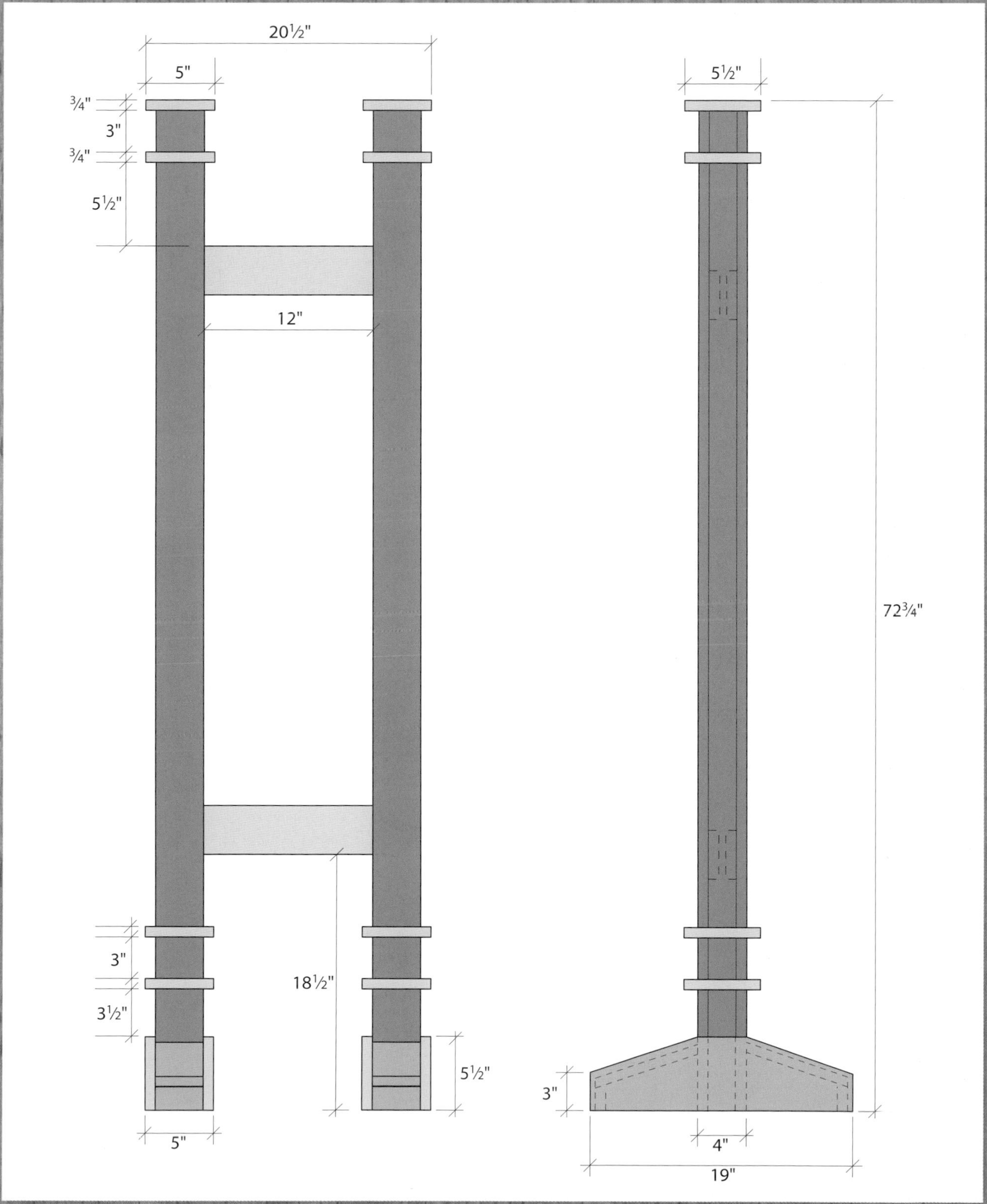
20½"
5"
¾"
3"
¾"
5½"
12"
3"
3½"
18½"
5½"
5"
5½"
72¾"
3"
4"
19"

To throw another stumbling block in the way; it's easier to mark the biscuit locations on the post pieces before attaching the cross beams. So, follow the photos at right to mark and cut your biscuit pockets. I spaced the locations about 12" apart, and kept the end pockets about 2" in from the ends of the parts.

Next, mark the locations for the cross beams, using the illustrations on the preceding page. I held the top beams 9¾" down from the top edge, and the second set, another 41" down from the first set.

HIDING UGLY SCREWS

I find 1⅝" coarse-thread drywall screws to be very effective for woodworking. Not pretty, but effective. The screws holding the cross beams in place are hidden inside the posts, so pretty isn't a concern here. Make sure to drill clearance holes wider in diameter than the diameter of the screw body. Makes things easier, and it will pull the joint tighter.

To make sure the cross beams stay in the right place while I screw them in place, a couple of fast-adjusting clamps work fine. (Clamps are something that are always in demand in a weekend shop, but I find a few of each type usually provides what I need.)

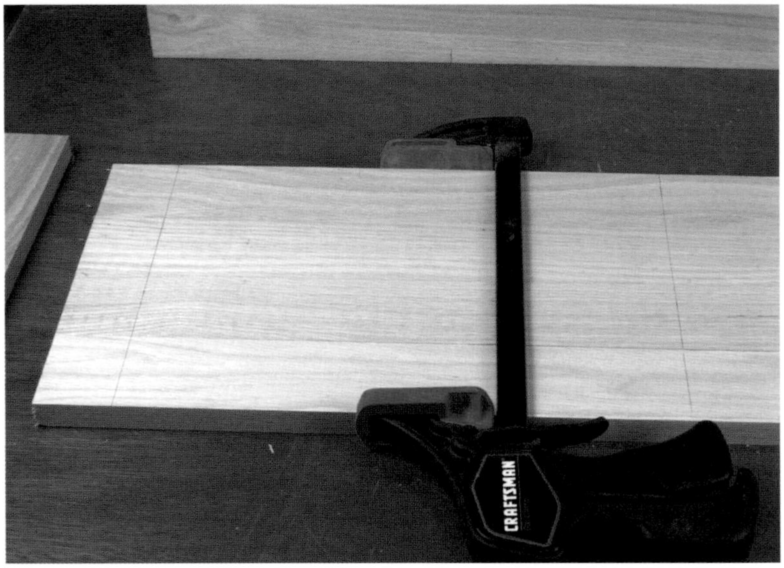

3 ... and then again on the outside face of the post's side pieces. A clamp here also keeps the four pieces properly aligned.

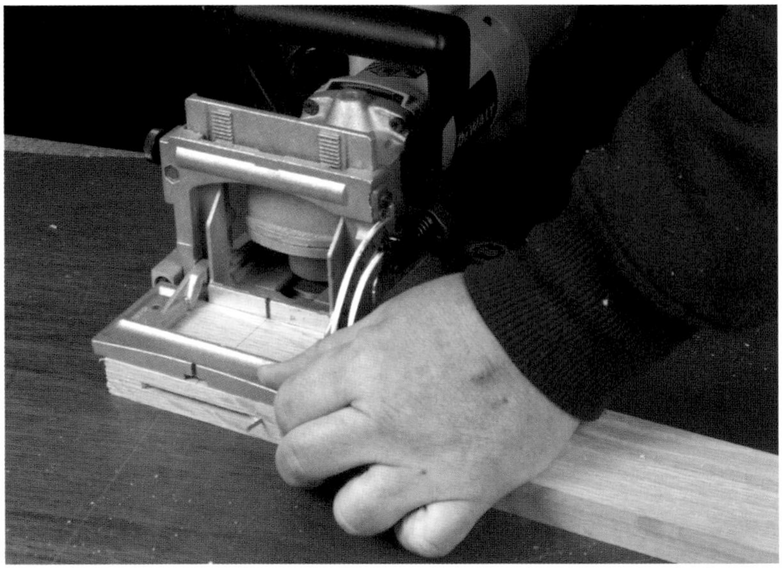

4 Line up your biscuit jointer and cut pockets on both edges of the side pieces.

5 Then cut pockets on the inside face of the posts fronts and backs.

6 Test your fit. Preferably the side face and the front edge will align perfectly, but that's not always possible. The next best thing is to have the edge extend slightly beyond the face. This makes it easier to plane or sand the surface flush.

7 Even though we've just done the joinery to build the posts, we need to step back a minute and screw the cross beams between the post sides first. Use a drill bit to make a clearance hole through the sides at the proper locations.

8 The screw heads won't be seen, but I used a countersink to get a little extra length and grab from the screws. I'm attaching the "face down" cross beams first to take advantage of the work surface to register the pieces flush.

I didn't use glue in this instance, and in fact there's not a whole lot of glue used in the project. If it's a long grain-to-long grain joint, then yes, glue is good. But if it's an inferior end-grain-to-long-grain joint, I'm more likely to make a gluey mess that will show up when I'm staining, than to gain any strength.

Working on a flat, level surface to build this project is very helpful. My inexpensive hollow-core door sitting on a couple of horses does just fine. Attach the cross beams that are "down" first. This will help to align the edges.

BOXING THE POSTS

With the cross beams screwed in place, it's time to build the posts. We've already got all our biscuit pockets cut, so it's a simple matter of not turning the hall tree over too many times. For the sake of the photos, I completed one post and then took photos as I assembled the second. But I'd recommend starting with the two "down" faces.

Put a bead of glue connecting the biscuit pockets on the inside joints, then add biscuits and tap the sides into place. Repeat the process with the outside two sides.

As you proceed, it's a good idea to check the length of your post pieces. While they were all cut to be the same length, things do move during a glue up. Preferably the top ends of the posts would be as perfectly aligned as possible. The tops will have a cap added, and not having to sand the end flush is a good thing. If the

9 Next, attach the second set of cross beams. I didn't bother to flip things over, I checked the flushness of the edge as I drove the screws home.

10 Now we're ready to build the posts. Run a bead of glue along the edge of the center side, then slip the face (with biscuits in place) under the side and tap it home.

11 The outside sides are next (as you may have noticed, I'm working on the second post here). Again, use just enough glue. The less clean-up necessary the better.

12 And finally, the second "face" piece is glued and tapped in place.

13 With all the pieces in place, it's time to see how many clamps you own. I had to use some mismatched clamps, and could only do one post at a time, but it works. Space the clamps about 12" apart, but check the gap as you go to make sure it's all pulled up tight.

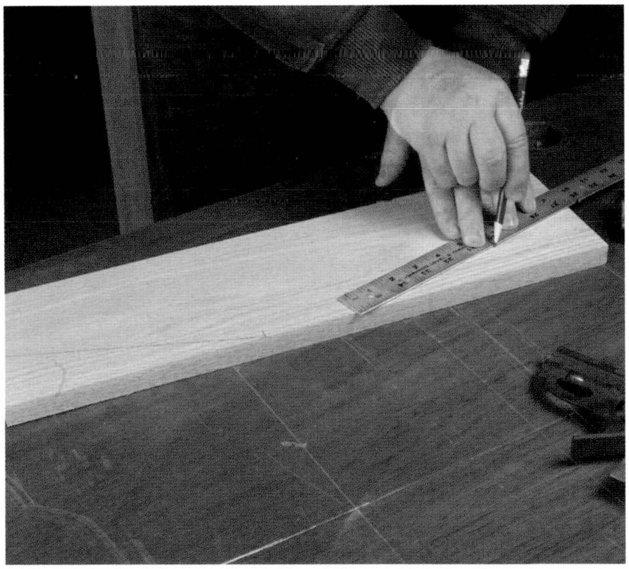

14 While the glue on the posts dries, move to the bases. First, mark the two slopes on the four base sides. Mark the 4" in both directions centered at the top of the sides. Then make a mark 2" up from the bottom of the sides on both ends. Then connect the dots.

bottoms of the posts are off a bit, we'll be hiding them inside the feet, and no one will know.

Finish assembling the posts by adding some more glue, a few more biscuits and the two final faces. Again, check your fit while things are still able to be moved a bit.

Now grab all the clamps at your disposal and glue the post sides together. If you need to glue one post at a time, no worries. Take your time and make sure the joints are good and tight.

MAKING IT STAND UP

You're now ready to move on to the bases. These are designed to look and feel stable. I've had a couple of comments that it gives the coat rack the look of a robot, so you may feel inclined to try your own hand at designing, if the bases aren't to your personal taste. All I know is when I put a bunch of winter coats on the rack, I don't want it tipping or leaning. I essentially built the bases around the posts, then screwed them in place to the posts. The slope of the bases helps soften what is already a somewhat blocky look.

I used biscuits to align all the pieces, and also avoided using any visible joinery. I did need to screw the bases to the posts, so I used a countersunk wood plug to hide the screws.

15 Now plug in your jigsaw and cut the slopes on all four sides. Remember, the cleaner the cut and the closer to the line, the easier the cleanup.

16 Speaking of the cleanup, I used my bench plane to smooth out the slopes. If you don't have a bench vise, a couple of wood clamps can substitute in a pinch.

17 Most of the joints on the base are long-grain-to-long-grain, but I wanted to use biscuits to align the pieces. Clamp the base together to mark for the biscuits and check the fit for the base top pieces and the end caps. You may want to bevel the ends of the base caps to match the slope of the base sides. It's a better finished look.

18 Make your biscuit cuts in the base pieces. To assemble, the first step is to glue the end caps to the base tops.

19 I pre-drilled and countersunk two holes in each base side, then glued the two assembled tops to one side.

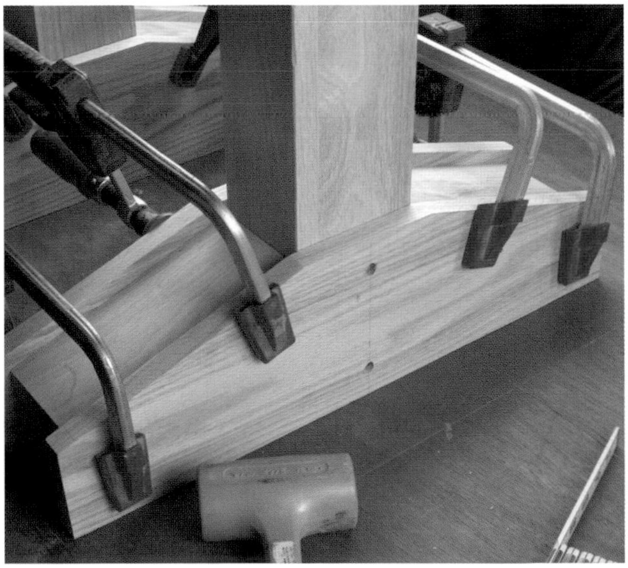

20 Place the assembled side around the post and glue the other side in place.

THE BANDS

Next step is the banding for the posts. What's it good for? Absolutely nothing, except to add some Frank Lloyd Wright prairie-style accents. It seems simple enough, just take some ¾" × ¾" banding (you can make your own, or buy it in the trim section of your home center store) and nail it in place. But fitting all the pieces and having them align correctly on the posts takes a certain amount of patience and accuracy. Take your time.

To complete the look, two square caps are nailed in place at the top of the posts.

AND THE FINISH

The finish for this piece was interesting. Most of Frank's prairie pieces went against the common darker finishes found on Art & Crafts pieces. His finishes were more a coloring of the wood, but a lighter brown. I went with a Minwax Golden Oak stain and a wipe-on polyurethane top coat. You may prefer to make your piece a little darker.

21 Double check the base in relation to the post using a square, then go ahead and screw the sides to the posts.

22 Put a little glue on the plugs and tap them into place over the screws.

23 The plugs won't exactly disappear, but after sanding, they'll add a finished touch and hide the screws nicely.

24 You're now ready to start the banding at the top of the posts. First measure down 3" from the top of the posts and make marks on all four sides. This will be the top of the banding.

25 To cut and fit the miters, start with one piece of banding mitered to 45°, and allow it to run long on the other end. Clamp this piece in place (no glue) and use it to mark the adjoining piece of banding. Cut the piece to length.

26 Add some glue to that piece …

27 ... and nail it into place. I had the advantage of a 23-gauge, micro-pinner, but a hammer and finish brads will work also.

28 Remove the clamp and your starter piece and follow the pattern around the post, marking the next piece, cutting it…

29 ...and nailing it in place.

30 Mark, cut and nail the third piece in place.

31 Finally mark the fourth piece (I hung on to my starter piece to use for the other banding sections), checking the fit carefully.

32 Then add some glue and nail it in place.

33 For a little extra strength, I tacked a nail in place through the miter into the adjoining banding piece. I repeated this for all the corners. This step is repeated on the opposite post, and then four more times at near the bottom of the posts. Take your time.

34 The top caps finish off the posts. Cut the cap to size and then align one edge of the cap with the banding below.

35 Align the adjoining edge of the cap and mark the location on the cap.

36 Finally, nail the cap at that corner. Check the opposite corner and complete the assembly.

BIG IDEAS
FOR...

MACKINTOSH TABORET

14

Charles Rennie Mackintosh (1868-1928) was a Scottish architect and designer who was influenced by the English Arts & Crafts Movement and designed a number of very distinctive furniture pieces. His work stands apart from the more strict designs found in much of the American Arts & Crafts designs, and I think that's why I find his work a pleasure to adapt. That table shown here is an adaptation of a table Mackintosh created for the Willow Tea Room in Glasgow, Scotland. The original was made of hickory, so poplar made a fine economical option for me. The upside-down tear drop cutout on my table was a fairly elaborate carving on the original. Not being a carver myself, I thought this a reasonable alternative. Please feel free to tackle a carving if you prefer.

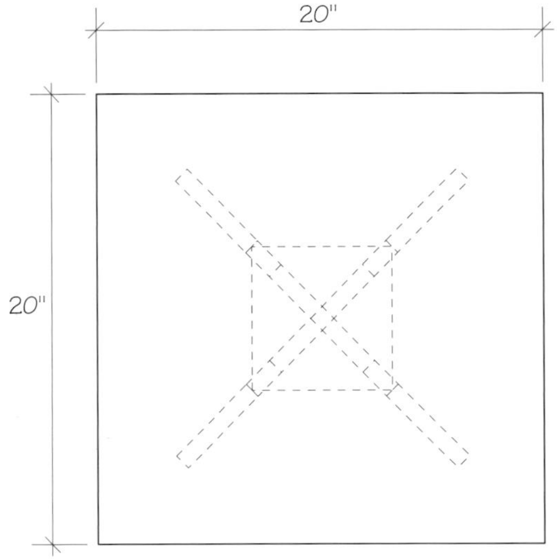

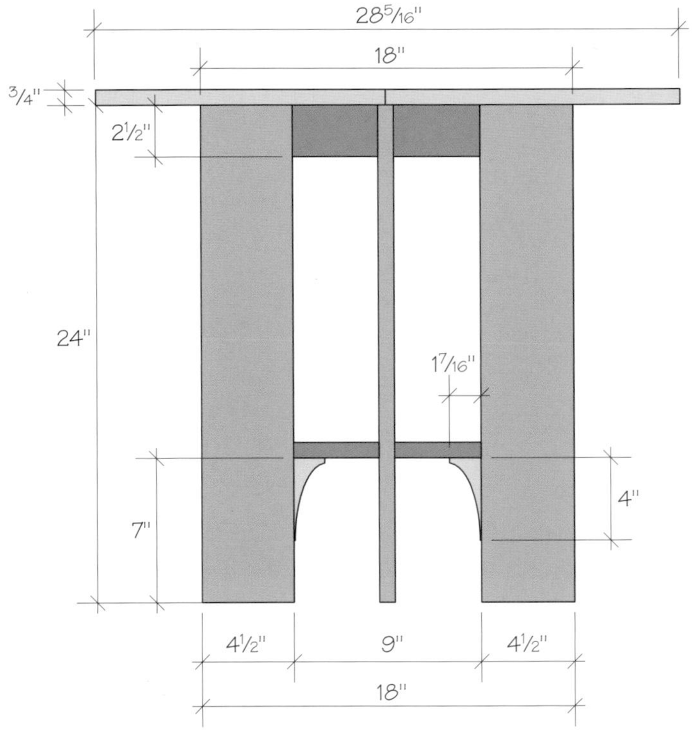

MACKINTOSH TABORET • INCHES (MILLIMETERS)

REFERENCE	QUANTITY	PART	STOCK	THICKNESS	(mm)	WIDTH	(mm)	LENGTH	(mm)
A	4	legs	poplar	3⁄4	19	4½	115	24	610
B	2	stretchers	poplar	3⁄4	19	2½	64	9	229
C	1	top	poplar	3⁄4	19	20	508	20	508
D	1	shelf	poplar	3⁄4	19	6⅜*	162	6⅜*	162
E	4	corbels	poplar	3⁄4	19	1½	38	4	102

*Allow extra for trimming to final size.

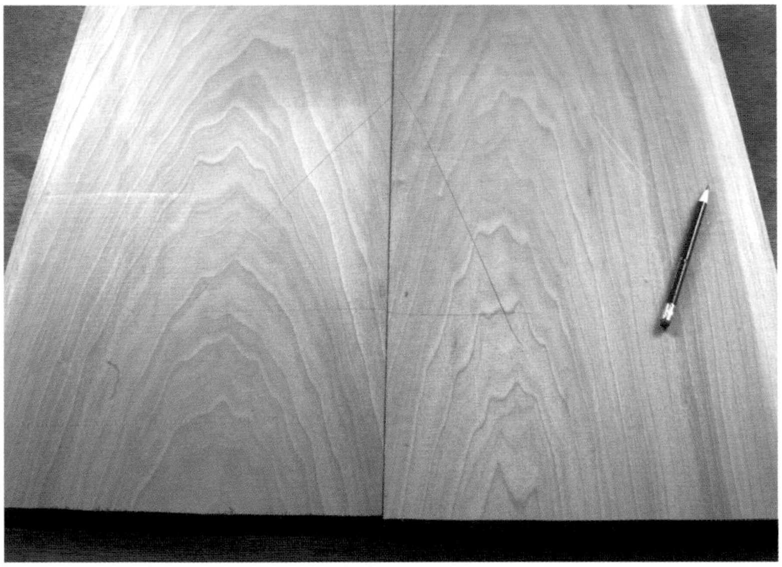

1 Start by finding the best figure match for the joint in your top. Poplar will not always offer an amazing match, but by using a single 1×8 board for the top, your chances are improved. Mark the joint once you've made your decision. A triangle shape shows board orientation quickly.

2 My factory edges weren't a wonderful match, but by clamping the two boards together (folding the two halves with both "good" sides facing out), a few swipes with a bench place improves the joint's fit.

SELECTING MATERIAL

Construction on the table begins with the top. Amazingly enough, I was able to get this entire table from a single 1×8×10' poplar board. This not only saved in material expense, but also allowed me to make the top with only one joint down the center.

Another advantage to the single board was the uniformity of the color of the poplar. As you may be aware, poplar can run the gamut from a dark purple, through green, brown and then on to white, all in a single board. As I intended to stain the table, I wanted to get the best color match I could, so the single board afforded me a fairly uni- from green for the entire table.

WORKING THE TOP

I started by finding the best figure match for the top. Again, the single board worked to my advantage, allowing me to come up with a grain match that looks almost like a book-matched piece. The term book matached comes from the appearance that the two halves of the top are nearly mirror images of one another, much like you would find if the top were folded at the joint (like a book), and then opened. It's a good look, and I was happy to come close to it.

To best align the figure, I ended up matching factory edges that were not square, or flat. So I needed to do a little work with my bench plane to get a good joint match. I then used biscuits to align the joint during glue-up (photos 1-5).

TEARDROP LEGS

While the glue on the top cures I moved on to the legs. Cut the legs to length, and then transfer the cutout design to each leg. I held the top of the pattern 4" down from the top of each leg, and centered on the width. I felt the height worked well to allow the cutout to be seen from a standing postion.

The cutout design on the legs is honestly one of the hardest parts of this project. Starting with a clean, even cut with the jigsaw makes cleaning up the shape afterward much easier.

I drilled a ⅜" hole at the point of the teardrop to give me clearance to insert the blade of my jigsaw. After that, it's just a steady hand.

HOLDING IT TOGETHER

Next we move on to some joinery. The two top stretchers of the table are held together in a X-shape using a half-lap joint created on one edge of each piece.

I used a table saw to create this joint, but you can also use a jigsaw. It's just more difficult to create as crisp a cut with the jigsaw, but if that's the only tool available, it'll do the job.

The half-lap provides strength to the leg section of the table, especially since the lower part is only connected through the shelf. Photos 9-12 detail the half-lap process using a standard table saw blade. If you happen to have access to a dado set, then you can shorten the process. But, for this single half-lap, the single

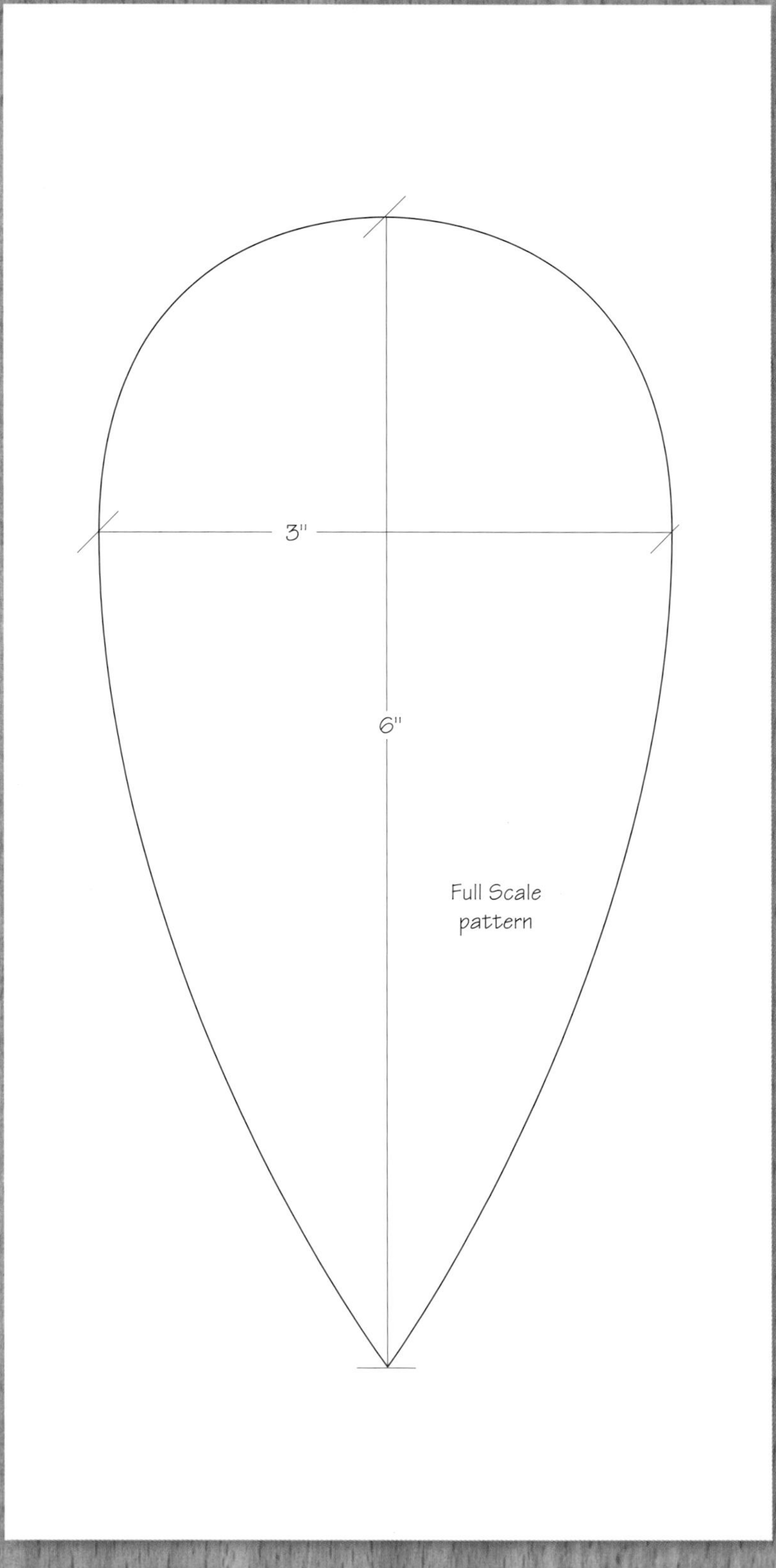

3 Test the joint after planing. You may need to repeat the process before you're happy with the match.

4 When you're happy with the joint, cut some biscuit slots. Because the joint is a long-grain-to-long-grain glue joint, strength isn't a concern, but I like using the biscuits to align the surfaces. This reduces the amount of sanding required.

5 I opted for four biscuits in the mating edges. Apply glue to one of the edges, and coat both sides of each biscuit before inserting. Then clamp the top together.

6 Use the pattern at the left to trace and then transfer the cutouts onto the leg surfaces. I used a jigsaw to make the cutout, but used a drill bit to create a starter hole. Choose a bit that is larger in diameter than the width of your jigsaw blade. Locate the starter hole close to the point of the cutout.

blade process works pretty efficiently also.

I do want to stress that this step leaves a lot of blade exposed without any guard. Because the cut is only part-way through the piece of wood, it's nearly impossible to make the cut with a guard in place. Be very careful, and pay attention to where your hands are place. I've added a taller piece of scrap pine to my miter gauge to help support the cut and to give me a larger surface to keep my hands further from the blade. Safety first, please.

CORBELS

One of the details of this table that caught my eye and makes it so much more than just a simple table are the small corbels, or brackets, that support the bottom shelf. You could easily argue that notching the legs for the shelf would have been fine, but the corbel's shape adds a pleasing sweep to the legs and supports the shelf in an elegant way. The corbels are simply blocks edge-glued to the legs, and then cut to shape using a jigsaw.

As I started to try and figure out what size radius I should use for the corbel (it's a pretty large radius, and my protractor isn't that large), I realized I could cheat and use the teardrop template for the corbel, too. By using the upper quarter of the teardrop pattern, I was able to quickly mark a nicely shaped corbel on each block.

7 Make your cut in as continuous a motion as possible. This means leaving the entire piece accessible, so I clamped my leg so it was hanging out over the edge of my work surface. If you're using an orbital jigsaw, using the lowest (straightest) setting to avoid over-cutting the underside.

8 Most jigsaw blades "favor" one side of the cut during a curve. This means the blade will move out of perpendicular with the cut. Check your cut to make as smooth a cut as possible, moving around the shape and finishing back at the point.

9 To create the half-lap joint, I set the height of the blade to the height of the joint and make a cut on the inside of the waste section. A miter gauge with a sacrificial back board makes this cut much easier.

10 I then make another cut to define the other side of the joint. Be careful moving to the next cut, allowing the wood to move completely clear of the blade before aligning the next cut. Kick backs are possible, so pay attention.

11 The rest of the cuts nibble away the wood between the first two cuts. Notch the second piece in the same manner, then check the fit. Make adjustments as necessary.

12 A good half-lap joint should be reasonably snug, but not so tight that you need to force the two halves together. The two pieces should fit flush to one another at the top and bottom.

ADDING CONTOURS

Next I cleaned up the cutout teardrop shapes with a rasp, file and sandpaper, and then decided to soften the edges further by using a ¼" roundover router bit in my trim router. This treatment also helped hide some of the blade marks from the jigsaw. I did this step before assembling the legs because the joinery is a little fragile until the table is assembled.

I liked the way the roundover bit worked in the cutout, but a test piece in the shape of the legs convinced me that the rest of the table should have edges softened only by hand sanding. Too much router work takes away from the crisp, straight lines that are an easily identifiable element in Arts & Crafts furniture.

PUTTING IT ALL TOGETHER

Next I assembled the legs using biscuit joinery where the legs meet the stretchers. A single biscuit at each joint is all that will fit, but a biscuit is important here. The joint is a long-grain-to-end-grain match, and as such is a poor glue joint for strength. And until the bottom shelf is attached to the corbels, the bases are pretty fragile U-shaped pieces.

THE HORIZONTAL PARTS

With the two leg halves drying, it's time to turn to the shelf and the top.

The shelf is a simple square, but will be a focal point of the table. Pay attention to the grain for this piece. It fits between the four legs, and requires four ¾"-

13 To create the corbels, I simply edge-glued a block of scrap to the lower part of each leg. By doubling up the gluing process I only needed one clamp for two legs. Keep the surfaces as flush to one another as possible to reduce sanding.

14 When the glue is dry, mark the curve from the teardrop pattern, starting down about ¼" from the top of the block. Then connect the end of the radius to the bottom of the leg in a gentle line. Get your jigsaw out and shape your corbels.

15 A roundover profile (use a clockwise motion with the router on an inside cut) on the edges of the cutouts makes them stand out a bit more, and also helps blend some of the rough edges from the jigsaw cut. I hate sanding, so any chance to reduce that task is a good one!

16 Join the stretchers to the legs using a single biscuit. I used a No. 10 biscuit that fit the stretcher width perfectly.

17 One clamp holds the assembly tight while the glue cures. By the way, make sure your two assemblies have the half-lap joints in the stretchers facing one up, and one down. Otherwise, oops!

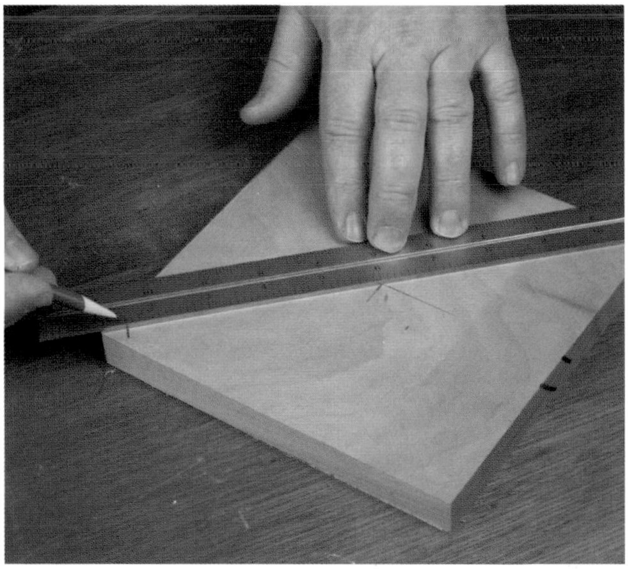

18 For a simple little shelf, it takes some accuracy to make the fit correct. The important dimension is the distance between the legs where the corners of the shelf meets the legs. Find the center of the shelf and then mark the distance required between the legs.

wide "flats" be cut at the corners to make the best fit against the inside edges of the table legs. And while I've given you the overall size of the shelf in the cutting list, you should double check the measurment between the legs to make sure you get an accurate fit.

The shelf is attached through the underside of the corbels. Be gentle with this step. Start with a clearance hole (I used a ⅛"-diameter bit) and then used a #6 × 1" screw to attach the shelf.

After squaring off the top to finished size, I gave the entire piece a good sanding (don't forget to ease the edges), and then applied a coat of Minwax Jacobean wood stain. A top coat of semi-gloss spray lacquer finished it off.

The last part is to attach the top to base. With solid wood, it's important to allow for seasonal wood movement across the width of a board. In this case, our top is likely to move, so I used a simple fastener mounted into the tops of the legs to allow wood movement.

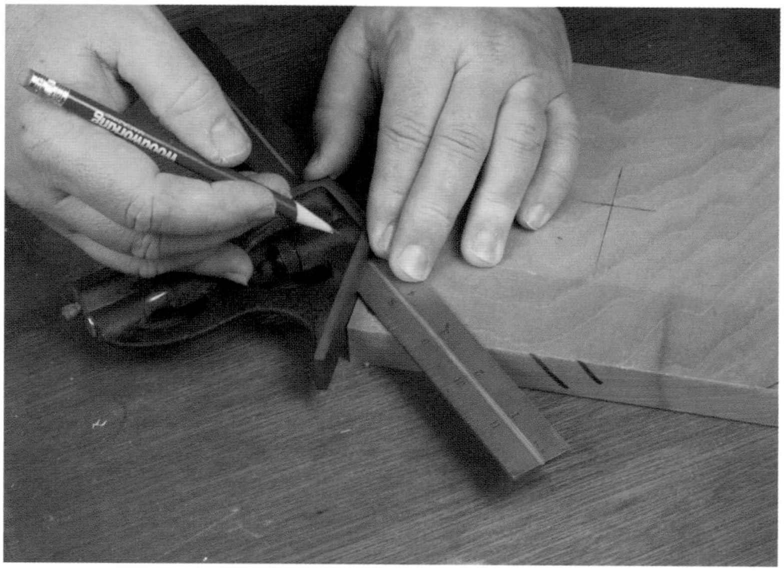

19 Use an adjustable square to mark the flats on the shelf corners, and then use the most convenient saw to cut the corners off the shelf.

20 To attach the shelf, I pre-drilled and countersunk screw holes in each of the corbels, up from the bottom of the leg. This hides the screws and adds a good bit of strength to the table.

21 To mount the base to the top, I use a figure-8 fastener available from Rockler. First, a depression is cut in the leg top using a Forstner bit larger in diameter than one side of the fastener. Only a little deeper than the thickness of the fastener, please.

22 To allow the fastener a little room to move from side-to-side with wood movement, I use a chisel to widen the mouth of the depression.

23 The fastener screws in place with everything flush to the top edge of the leg. Repeat the process for each leg.

24 Lastly, the base is screwed to the top. Simple, and efficient.

NEW:BUNGALOW
NEW:BUNGALOW:
ARTS & CRAFTS FURNITURE
GREENE&GREENE:MASTERWORKS

LIMBERT BOOKCASE

15

This "bookcase" is only about three-feet tall, so it's actually a magazine stand. That's what they called it in the catalog at least. The No. 300 magazine stand is built to the same proportions as shown here, and amazingly enough, in every photo I can find of an original piece there are wood buttons on the sides, hiding screw holes. That doesn't mean cutting corners on joinery, it means Charles Limbert was ahead of his time.

This magazine stand was obviously designed to be pre-finished in the factory, and then shipped unassembled (flat) to the store or customer. Sixteen screws and some buttons glued in place and the stand was ready to fill. Ikea, eat your heart out!

Even though there was a history of visible joinery on this stand, I didn't feel like using buttons. Instead I opted for my well-used countersink bit and wooden plugs. I think it enhances the look even further.

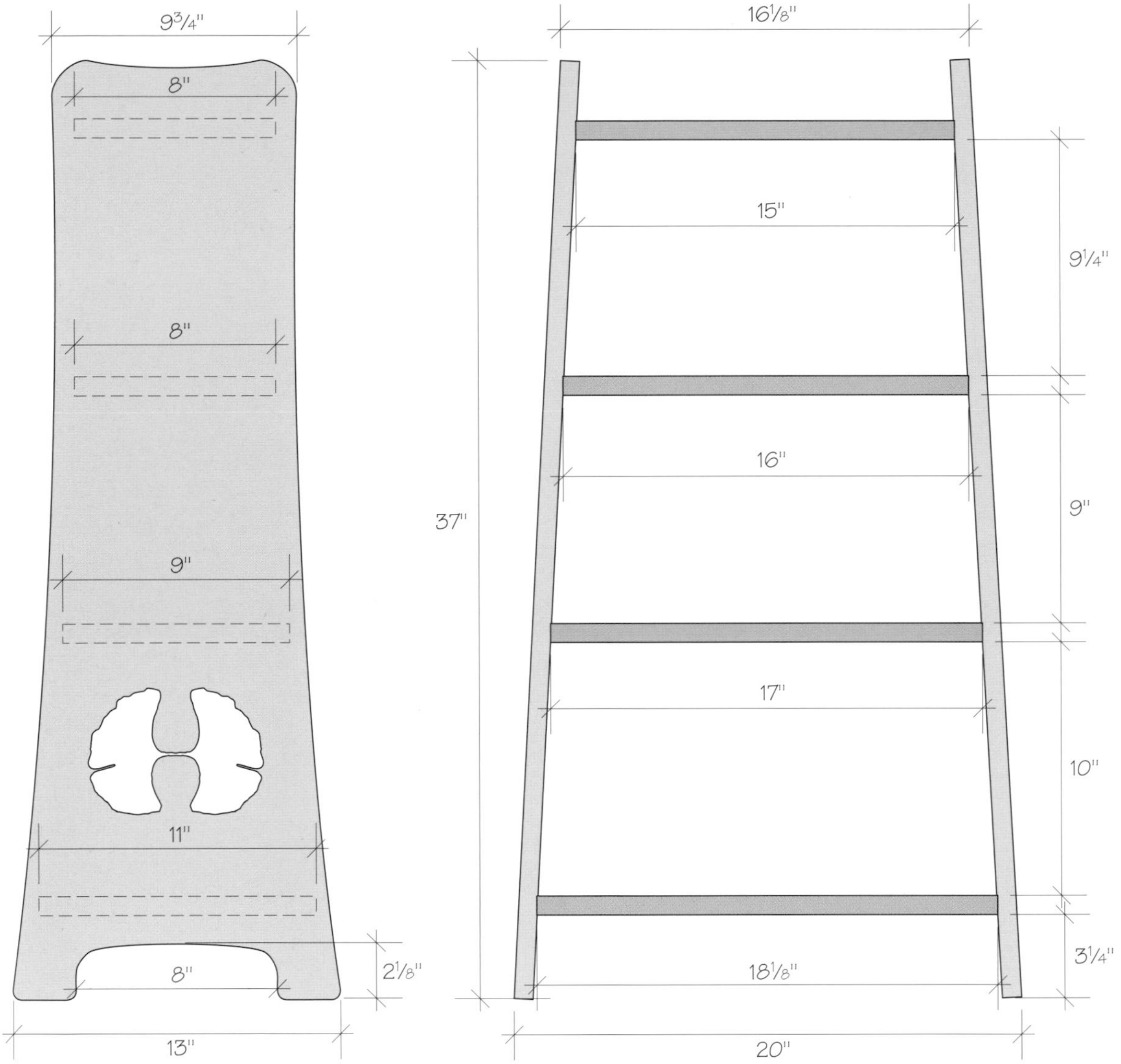

LIMBERT BOOKCASE • INCHES (MILLIMETERS)

REFERENCE	QUANTITY	PART	STOCK	THICKNESS	(mm)	WIDTH	(mm)	LENGTH	(mm)
A	2	sides	oak	¾	19	13	330	37	940
B	1	shelf	oak	¾	19	11	279	18⅛	460
C	1	shelf	oak	¾	19	9	229	17	432
D	1	shelf	oak	¾	19	8	203	16	406
E	1	shelf	oak	¾	19	8	203	15	381

1 Work starts by transferring the side pattern from the dimensioned plan on page 146 to one side of the glued-up side blanks. While you could try and size-up the pattern on a copier, I found it easier to count the squares and make the marks on the wood itself. Connecting the dots gets you close to the shape, but don't be afraid to wander a little as you cut.

2 Cut one half of the shape on this side, then flip that side onto the second side piece and trace the pattern on both edges. After making those two cuts, use the second side piece to trace the pattern onto the last straight edge on the first piece and cut it to shape. Magic. All four sides match!

I also made a change on a whim. The original No. 300 stand included a double-D cutout (two capital Ds back to back, spaced about 1" apart) on the lower third of each side. It's a nice look to jazz up the piece, but while walking through my backyard I caught the sun shooting through the leaves on my ginkgo tree and I was inspired. My version of this stand now has a cutout of stem-to-stem ginkgo leaves. I think it looks pretty cool, and while using a jigsaw to cut the shapes leaves a rougher edge, it looks fine on a leaf (so less sanding!).

I did keep to oak for the project, but the home center stores don't sell white oak, red oak only. The first step is to glue up the sides and shelves from 1×8 and 1×6 pieces. Try to pick the wood grain and color carefully while in the store. Cut the pieces to length (slightly oversize to allow for trimming), paying attention to grain match as you go.

MAKE THE SIDES

With the sides glued up, lay out the side pattern from the dimensioned diagram on page 146. With the points from the grid in place, it's just connect the dots. Allow a little fluidity in your drawing.

Next, grab your jigsaw and start cutting. Use relief cuts along the way to help with the curved sections. When you have the first side roughed out, use that shape to mark the second side.

With both sides rough cut, clamp the two together and go

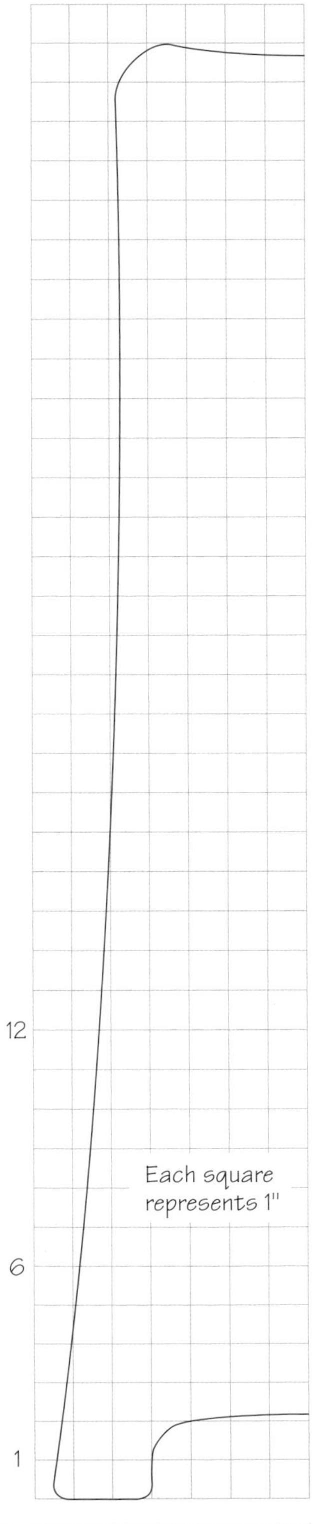
12
Each square represents 1"
6
1

3 Use the full-size pattern of the ginkgo leaf (at left) to draw the pattern on one side piece, add the details for the base cut out from the illustrations, then be a little creative with the stems of the leaves.

4 I'm not going to lie to you, this cut-out took about 30 minutes (one side) take your time, be safe and it'll look great.

to work with your random orbit sander, and wood files to clean up the jigsawn edges and make the two sides mirror each other in shape.

ADDING THE LEAF

Next, use the full-size plan of the ginkgo leaf to lay out the cutouts on one side. I just laid the shape on the side and turned it till I thought it looked nice, then did the same for the mirror image. Using the side pattern on page 146, I also marked the shape of the base cutout on each side. The fun part was then free-hand drawing the stem reaching up from the base. Remember to allow enough room to get the jigsaw blade in and out of the cut.

As with a couple of other cutouts on some of the projects, if you have a band saw, you may want to opt for that machine to make this cutout a little easier. That said, I enjoyed the process with a jigsaw.

With the sides detailed, take the time to finish sand the inside face of the two sides with your random orbit sander, breaking the sharp edges with sandpaper.

ADDING THE SHELVES

Using the illustration on page 144, locate the positioning for the top and bottom shelves on each side. Hold up on the two middle shelves for a moment. When you have the locations determined, use your countersinking drill bit to make two screw holes in each side for the top and bottom shelves.

Take the clamps off the glued up shelves, and cut the three upper shelves to width (the bottom shelf should already be at finished width). I used my bench top table saw for this, cutting from both sides of each shelf to leave the center joint in the center.

Next, cut the upper and lower shelves to the lengths given on the illustration. All of the shelves will have a 3° angle on each end, which will give the stand it's taper.

Start with the upper and lower shelves first, so you will have a chance to double-check the needed length for the two middle shelves.

Screw the lower shelf in place between the two sides. The shelves are evenly spaced from front to back. Then stand the piece up on your work surface and screw the top shelf in place as well.

Now look to the illustrations to determine the height of the two middle shelves, and take the measurement across the inside of the stand. Feel free to adjust the two middle shelf heights to best meet your needs.

Then cut the shelves, drill the countersunk holes and screw the shelves in place.

Now glue the wood plugs in place, wait for the glue to cure, then finish sand the whole thing.

I used Minwax's English Chestnut wood stain to color the piece and then topped it off with a few coats of semi-gloss spray lacquer.

5 Each shelf is held in place with plugged screws. I used two, per side, per shelf.

6 The end of each shelf is cut to length with a 3° angle. The angles should be mirrors of one another, not parallel. This allows the shelf to taper on the sides. I was able to use my miter saw to do this, but yours may not have a long enough cut for all the shelves. You can use a circular saw with the base set to 3° as another alternative.

7 Start the assembly with the lower shelf, screwing both sides to the shelf.

8 Stand the piece up and screw the top shelf in place.

9 Double check the measurement for the two middle shelves, then cut them to length and screw in place.

10 Wood plugs instead of buttons. A more civilized approach, I think.

HILL HOUSE TABLE

16

This hall table, designed by Charles Rennie Mackintosh, has been in the back of my mind since I first saw it in photos of the Hill House, in Helensburgh, Scotland. The original is a beautiful aged dark-wood (oak?). It had been my intention to make the piece sometime, but over the years I'd never had a hall worthy of the table. So consider me quite surprised that now, finally getting the chance to make the table, it's made of poplar and assembled with screws!

I adjusted the overall size of the piece, shrinking it slightly to accommodate today's home sizes. The original piece included a flat drawer centered in the apron. In keeping with the simpler construction approach, I opted to exclude the drawer, but you may feel inclined to add it back in.

While the piece is a painted piece, because it's function is for indoor use, the paint should be more of a lacquered finish. Because of this, I opted to use poplar for the base, and a birch plywood top. These woods will give a better sub-surface for the "lacquer".

ANXIOUS FOR LEGS

Start by cutting the six legs, and the four "apron" pieces to length. The apron pieces are assembled with pocket screws to form a rectangle. While it's a simple rectangle, all the measurements for the rest of the table are based on that first rectangle, so make your corners square. To hide the joints of the box behind the front legs, make sure the longer pieces are assembled between the shorter end pieces.

I was looking forward to getting into detailing the legs, and started to work on the side tapers of the first leg. As I was laying out the sides and thinking toward the cutting part, I realized I was about to loose the "square" edges that would be handy when laying out the square cutout locations. I went ahead and marked the tapered edges, but before any cutting I also marked the locations of the squares on each leg. Use the dimensions given in the illustration at the right to determine the location of the squares.

I was then ready to use my jigsaw to taper the legs, cutting slightly outside the line to allow a few clean-up passes with my bench plane.

1 Four of the six legs of this table attach to the center box, so that's a good place to start. The legs will hide the joints at the front, so I allowed the ends to run through, attaching the longer front and back to the ends using pocket screws. First cut the pockets...

2 ...then screw the box together. Square is good!

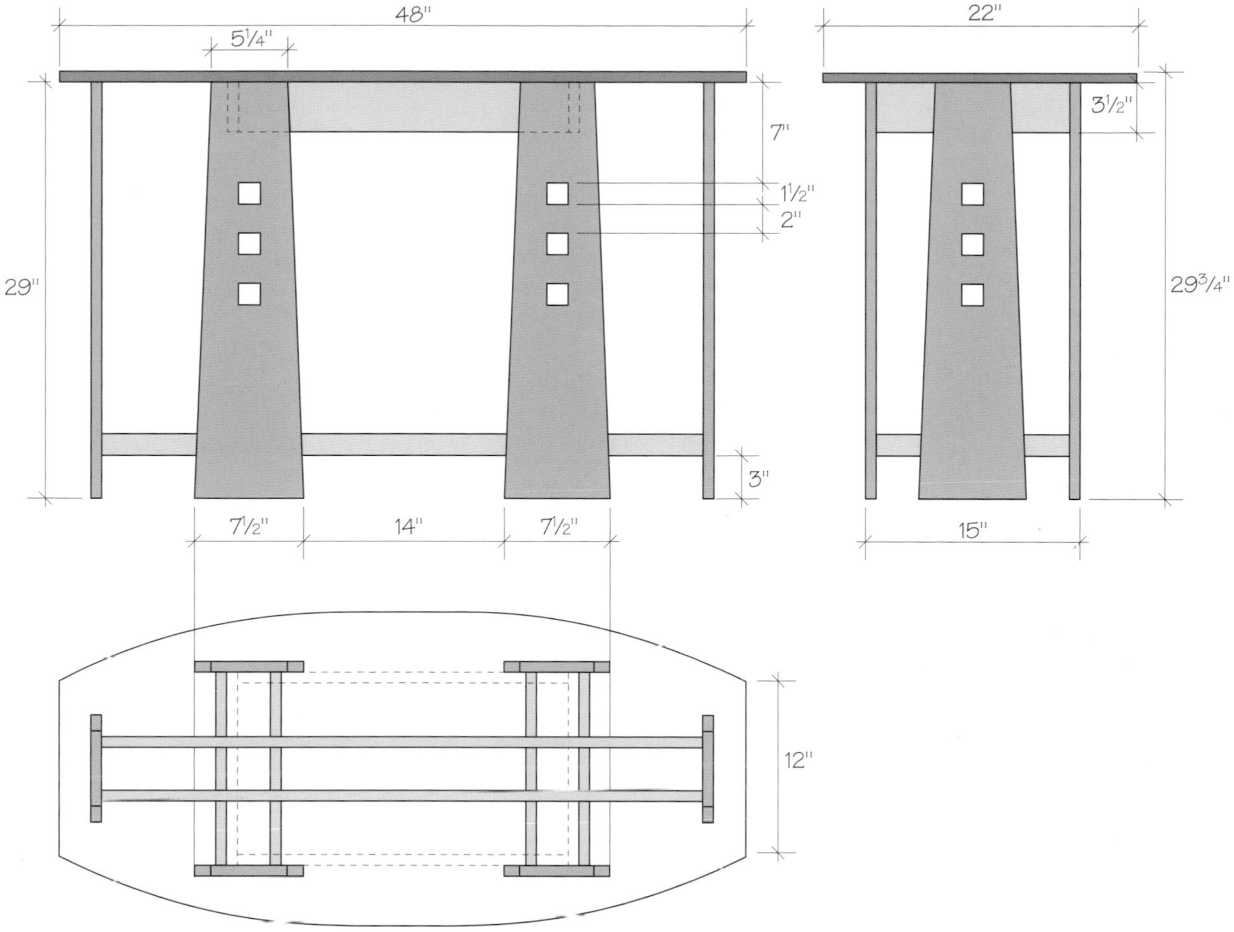

HILL HOUSE TABLE • INCHES (MILLIMETERS)

REFERENCE	QUANTITY	PART	STOCK	THICKNESS	(mm)	WIDTH	(mm)	LENGTH	(mm)
A	6	legs	poplar	$^3/_4$	19	$7^1/_2$	191	29	737
B	2	stretchers f/b	poplar	$^3/_4$	19	$3^1/_2$	89	23	584
C	2	stretchers sides	poplar	$^3/_4$	19	$3^1/_2$	89	$13^1/_2$	343
D	2	stretchers	poplar	$^3/_4$	19	$4^1/_2$	115	42	1067
E	4	stretchers	poplar	$^3/_4$	19	$3^1/_2$	89	$13^1/_2$	343
F	1	top	plywd	$^3/_4$	19	22	559	48	1219
		veneer tape	birch						

TOUGH SQUARES

Then I went back to focusing on the cutout squares. I first drilled access holes in the opposite corners of each square, staying slightly inside the edges of the square. I then used my jigsaw to cut sweeping arches near the corner, but not cutting straight in. I did this in both directions until the waste piece dropped free. I then went back and cleaned up each corner.

I won't lie to you. No matter how carefully you cut out the squares, there is going to be a fair bit of cleanup necessary (using chisels and files) to get the cutouts looking fairly crisp. Take your time and work through them.

BOTTOM STRETCHERS

Next are the 1×2 stretcher pairs at the bottom of the table. Cut the two long and four short stretchers to length. It's a smart idea to double check that the short stretchers are the same dimension as the width of the apron stretchers, front-to-back.

Then follow the layout dimensions in the diagram and carefully lay out the half-lap locations on the crossed stretchers. I oriented my layout so that when viewed from above the long stretchers ran through, and intersected the short stretchers. This places the notches on the long stretchers on the bottom edge, and on the top edge for the short stretchers.

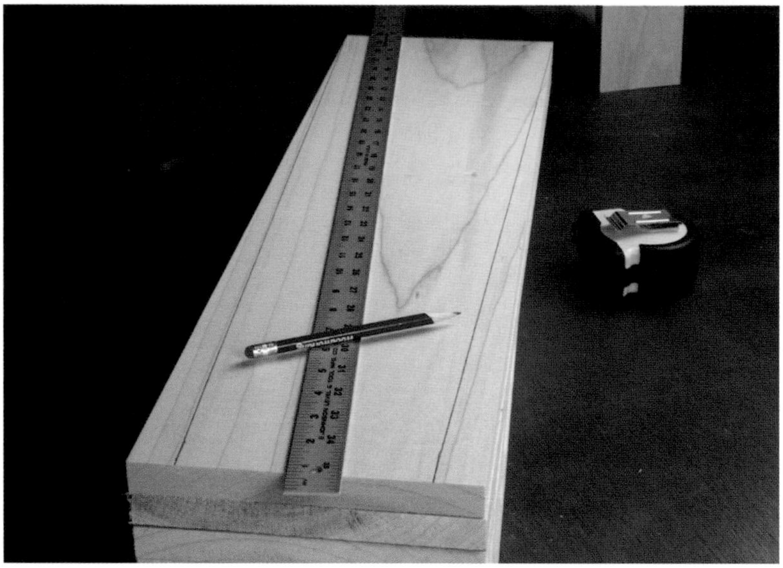

3 Using the illustrations, mark the tapers on the six legs, but don't cut them yet.

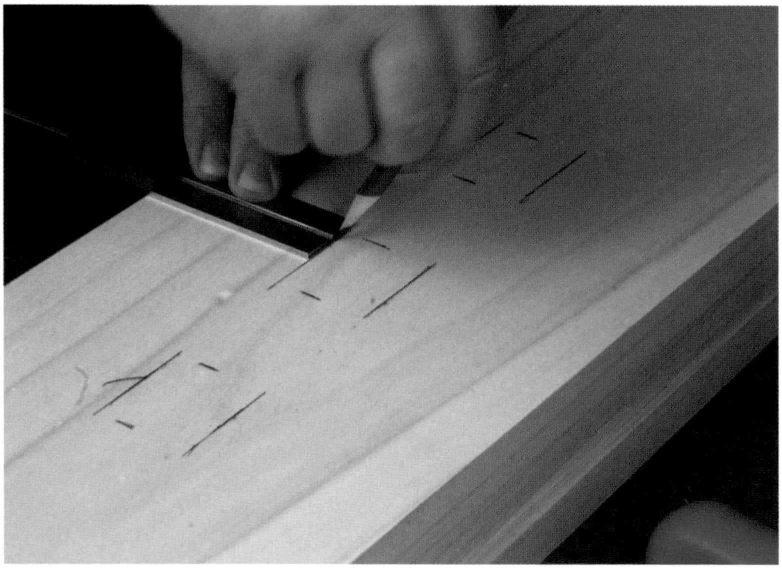

4 Check the locations for the square cut-outs on the illustrations, and then transfer them to the faces of the legs.

5 Go ahead and mark out the complete shapes of the squares.

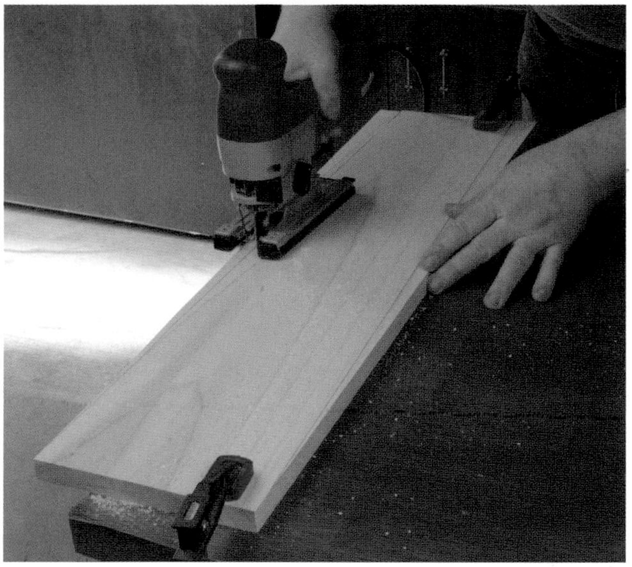

6 Now use the jigsaw to cut the tapers on the sides of the legs. Stay just wide of the lines and then use a bench plane to clean up the edges. I planed them in pairs (left front-and-back, right front-and-back, and two ends) in case there were any variations.

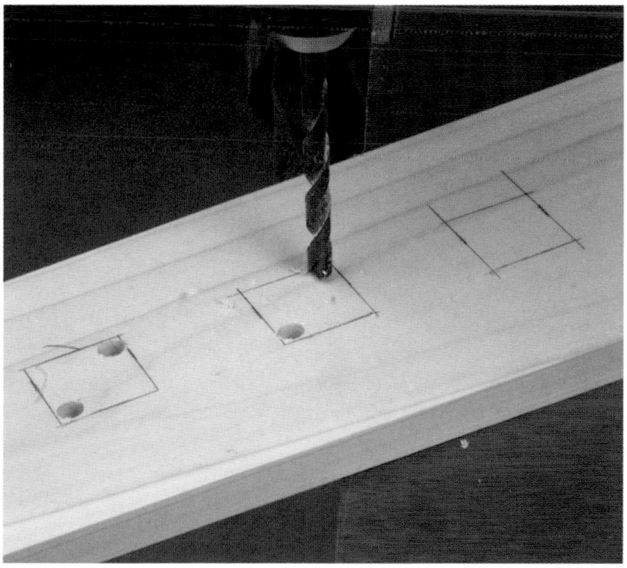

7 Now back to the squares. Make clearance holes for the jigsaw blade by first drilling with a drill bit. Don't drill too close to the corners.

8 Then cut away the waste areas of the squares using the jigsaw. Take it slow, and keep a close eye out for any blade deflection.

Check the fit of the entire grid, adjusting with a file to make it snug. You don't want too tight a fit, or you may crack the joint when assembling.

CREATING A LATTICE

The stretchers are held in place against the legs using screws inserted through the legs and into the ends of the stretchers.

The stretchers are positioned with the bottom edges 3" up from the bottom of each leg. The half-lap grid holds the stretchers approximately 4½" wide (outside dimension). So, to locate the screw locations, mark the center of each leg on the bottom edge, and then measure out 1⅞" in each direction. Make marks at these two locations, then measure up 3¾" from the bottom, and you will have your two screw locations on each leg. Pre-drill and countersink the holes. These dimensions locate the screws at the center (width and thickness) of each stretcher.

A thorough sanding on all the pieces is now in order. Even though the table will receive a black, painted finish, it will be a thin finish and the wood's grain (and any defects in the wood), will show through.

A BIG PUZZLE

I started assembly by building the stretcher grid and then screwing the two end legs to the long stretchers. I then added the face legs, working in pairs along the short stretchers.

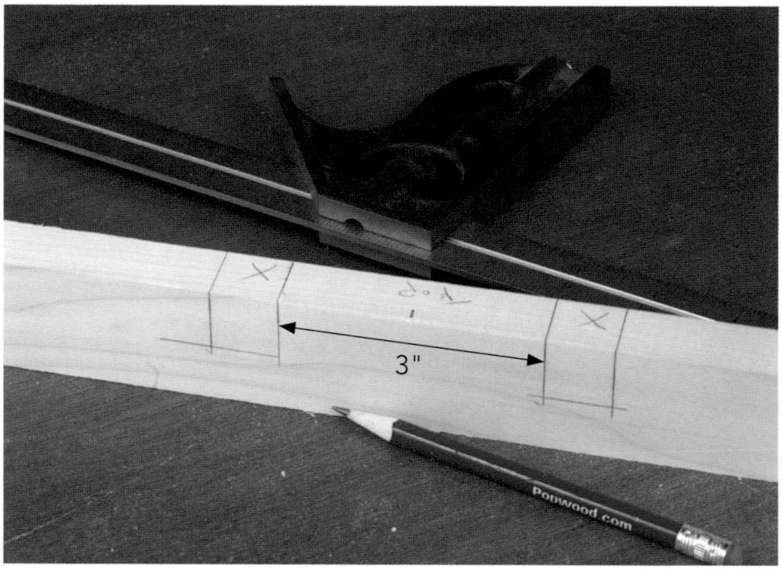

9 You're now ready to move on to the grid stretchers at the bottom of the piece. Mark the notches according to the illustrations, creating 3" squares at the meeting points.

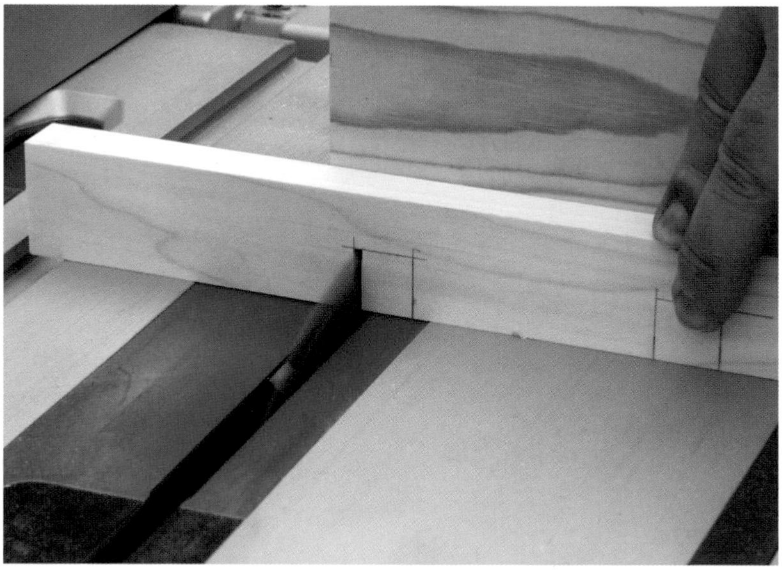

10 I used my table saw to make the notches, first defining one side...

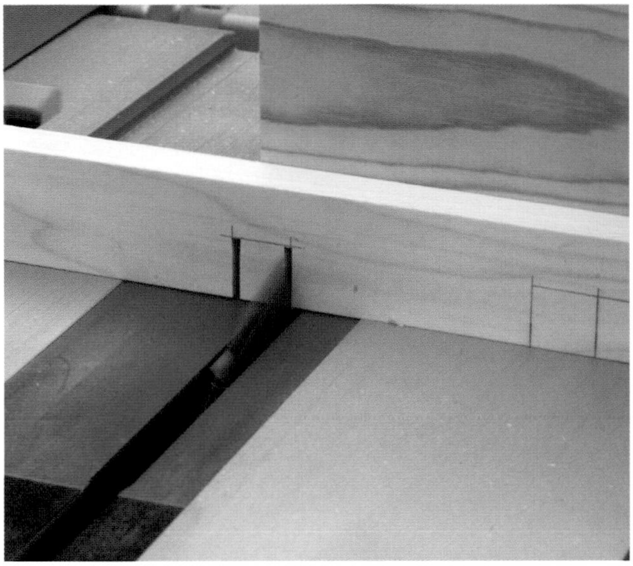

11 ...then the opposite side...

12 ...then nibbling away the wood between. Do this for all the notches.

13 You're ready for a little fitting assembly. Mark the location for the screw holes that will attach the legs to the bottom stretchers. I used my countersinking pilot bit to make the holes.

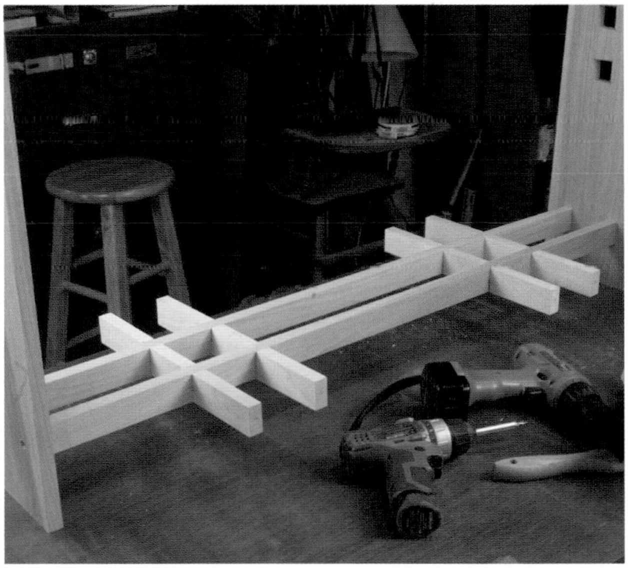

14 With the stretcher grid lightly assembled, screw the two end legs in place. With the whole thing sitting on a flat surface, go ahead and attach the front and back legs, paying attention to the fit of the stretcher notches, and making sure the six legs sit flat.

Manuevering all the pieces can be a little tricky, but take your time, work on a flat surface, and it'll all work out fine.

When everything was in place, I carefully incised (not pencil, in case paint covered anything up) letters on the top edge of the pieces to identify which pieces belonged together. Why? Well I decided that it would be much easier to put a coat or two of finish on the inside surfaces of the base pieces while the pieces were separated. So I disassembled the base, and started with a coat of flat black spray paint to use as a "primer" base coat. When dry, I sanded the painted surface with steel wool, then applied a second coat of paint.

AND THE TOP

To lay out the top shape, I've included a scaled drawing on page 159 to help you mark out the curve on a template piece. You only need one corner of the drawing to create the template, but I wanted to show how the "flats" of the top correspond to the curves.

With the pattern transfered to the four corners of the top, you're ready to run the jigsaw. Keep it smooth and steady and cut wide of the line to allow for smoothing out the edge. Clean up the edges with sandpaper and a file.

While I was working with a pretty good grade of plywood, I knew the edges of the plywood wouldn't be pretty under black paint. The simple solution was to add iron-on edge banding to

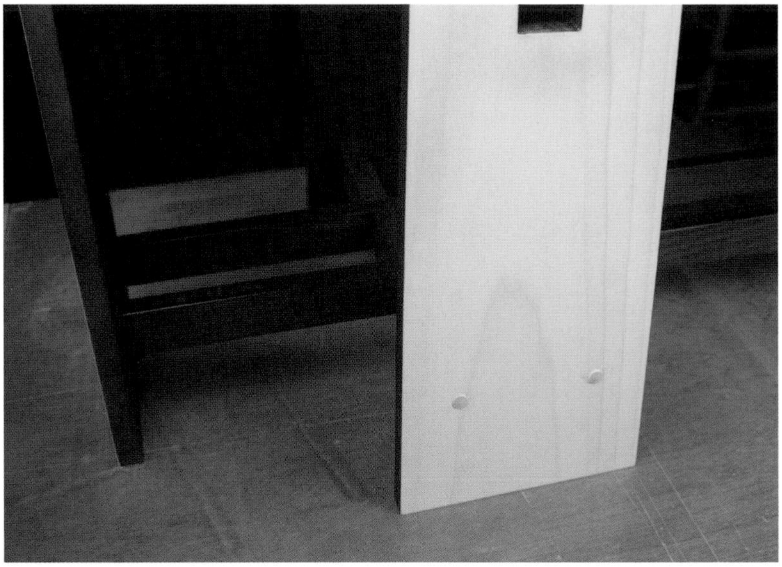

15 At this point I disassembled the table, marking all the leg and stretcher locations. Why? Because I didn't want to try and spray paint the insides of the table while it was assembled. After sanding, the painting went much easier with everything laying flat. Then I reassembled the frame and plugged the holes. The upper box was then screwed to the legs from the inside of the box.

16 The top was held in place using figure-8 shaped table hardware. For more detail on installing this hardware, see page 141.

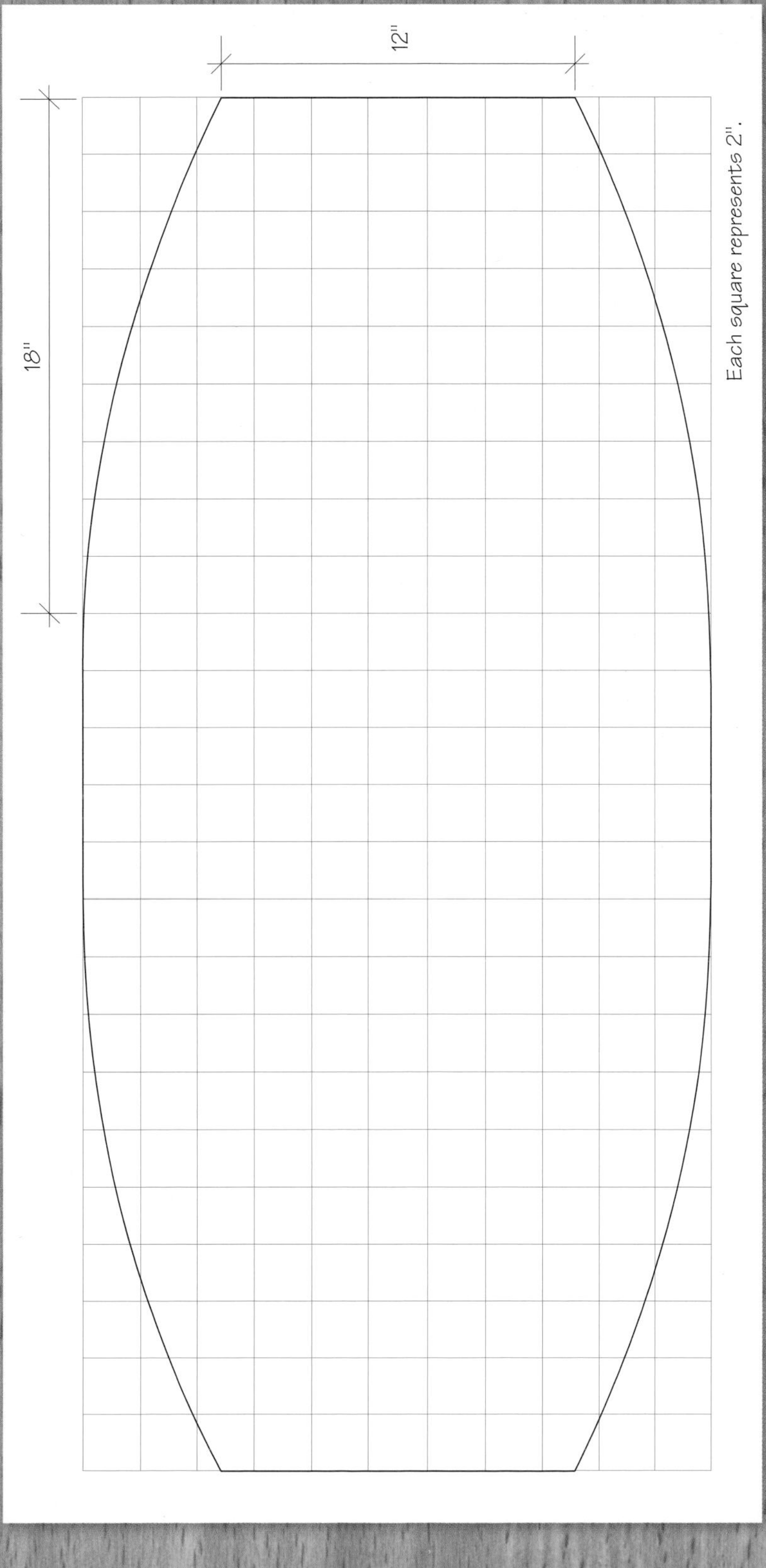

all four edges. The edge banding provides a good base surface for the sprayed finish, and blends with the textures of the other surfaces.

REASSEMBLE AND FINISH

When the paint on the base is dry, put all the pieces back together. Then plug the pair of screw holes in each leg. Sand the plugs flush and give the outside surfaces a once-over with sandpaper.

Spray two base coats on the outside surfaces and then follow with two-to-three coats of gloss black paint. Those coats proved adequate for the base, but I added a couple of coats of a clear gloss finish to the top to add depth and protection.

The last step is to fasten the top. I used figure-8 top-fastening hardware from www.rockler.com to mount the top.

Not too shabby for plywood, poplar and paint.

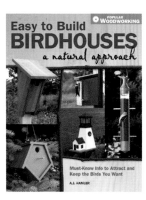